STUDY OUT THE LAND

STUDY OUT THE LAND

Essays by

THOMAS KING WHIPPLE

Who are you indeed who would talk or sing to America?
Have you studied out the land, its idioms and men?
—WALT WHITMAN, *Leaves of Grass*

Essay Index Reprint Series

BOOKS FOR LIBRARIES PRESS
FREEPORT, NEW YORK

INTERNATIONAL STANDARD BOOK NUMBER:
0-8369-2088-0

LIBRARY OF CONGRESS CATALOG CARD NUMBER:
76-134158

PRINTED IN THE UNITED STATES OF AMERICA

This Volume, Among Others Thus Specially Designated, Is
Published in Commemoration of the
SEVENTY-FIFTH ANNIVERSARY
of the Founding of the University of California

Acknowledgments

FOR PERMISSION to include in the present volume eight essays previously published, due acknowledgment is made to the original publishers and holders of the copyrights: for "Poetry and Morals," to the Regents of the University of California; for "Machinery, Magic and Art," and "Jack London— Wonder Boy," to *The Saturday Review of Literature;* for "The Myth of the Old West," to *The New Freeman* and *The Argonaut;* for "Dos Passos and the U.S.A.," to *The Nation;* for "Steinbeck: Through a Glass, Though Brightly," and "Literature in the Doldrums," to *The New Republic;* "Aucassin in the Sierras" is reprinted from *The Yale Review,* copyright Yale University Press, by permission of the Editors.

Contents

T. K. Whipple

BY EDMUND WILSON

I FIRST knew T. K. Whipple in the winter of 1912–13. He was a senior at Princeton and editor of *The Nassau Literary Magazine,* and I was a freshman contributor. The *Lit* had been rather in eclipse up to the time that T. K. (whom the campus called "Teek") had taken command of it the year before. Robert Shafer, since known as a critic and a follower of Paul Elmer More, was, I believe, the first editor in a series that represented a new period of literary activity at Princeton—the first since the early 'nineties, the days of Booth Tarkington and Jesse Lynch Williams. Whipple took over from Shafer, and the succeeding boards included John Peale Bishop, Hamilton Fish Armstrong, Isador Kaufman, W. Stanley Dell, Raymond Holden, F. Scott Fitzgerald, John Biggs, Jr., and myself. Among the contributors were Keene Wallis and A. O'Brien-Moore. Up to the time of Whipple's editorship the *Lit* had had the existence of a mouse that lurked timidly in a crevice of the college life. I remember Teek's telling me of the hopelessness with which they used to canvass the college rooms for subscriptions. The freshmen would buy tiger pictures, but they knew from the demeanor of the *Lit* people that the magazine was not taken seriously.

In the new era the *Lit* came to life. It made connections
with the other college activities: *The Princetonian* and the
Triangle Club; and at the same time it defended with boldness positions that were antagonistic to both official and
undergraduate opinion. We engaged in sharp controversies
with *The Princetonian* over the problems of the curriculum
and academic freedom, and there was a moment, under the
editorship of John Bishop, when Bishop's poetry—which
seemed very "modern"—became an issue on the campus almost comparable to the fight over the eating-club system.
We had an awfully good time out of the *Lit* and got some
excellent practice in writing and being read—for which
courses in "creative writing" had not yet at that date become
necessary; and we were usually able to cut at the end of the
year a melon which yielded each one of us a slice of about
fifty dollars. Teek Whipple, who had stayed on at the Graduate School after his graduation in 1913, had been with us
through all this period. He had helped and advised, and he
had written in his limpid and witty prose; and he had thus
given the whole evolution a continuity it would not otherwise have had. He had somehow established the mental
atmosphere in which the *Lit* was growing, and he continued
to water its roots.

Not that he was in the least a promoter or the kind of
man who likes to pull strings. He was a long-legged, loose-
jointed fellow, with pale blond hair and a Missouri drawl,
whose expression, with its wide grin, was at once sad and

droll. His manner and movements seemed languid when he was lounging on a window seat or Morris chair; but when one saw him striding the campus, hump-shouldered and hands in pockets, one felt in him a purposive independence. All that he did he did unobtrusively, but definitely and with conviction. In some ways he was remarkably mature for an American undergraduate. His enthusiasm for our Princeton humanism—by which I mean the tradition of, say, Lionel Johnson, a great favorite of T. K.'s at this time, not the Humanism of Babbitt and More—burned in an air that was dryer than the rather humid and dreamy atmosphere that tended to beglamour our ideas: an air of disillusioned common sense; and he seemed sure in the decisions of his judgment and taste as few men at college do. I remember it as characteristic of him that when I told him I was reading *Marius the Epicurean* and began to grope for phrases to express my mixed feelings about it, he said at once that it "would be a good book if it were not so badly written." And his devotion to literature was never dilettante-ish, as it is likely to be with undergraduates, nor did it ever become a matter of routine, as it is likely to do with professors: it was something fundamental to his life. He presented an unusual combination of Princetonian and Middle Westerner—of pleasantry, casualness, and elegance with homeliness, simplicity, and directness. Though he was not intellectually the most energetic or imaginatively the most brilliant of the group, he had something that is very rare and a little hard to define. He diffused

a quiet kind of light that accompanied him like a nimbus.
You were always glad to see him; you always knew the glow
was there; and in that medium the *Lit* revived.

T. K. and I, when I got to be editor for the year of 1915–16,
worked together in renovating the magazine and laying for
it a firmer base. We changed the type and format, as new
editors almost invariably do, and we gave it a permanent
cover, with an owl and the motto from Horace so often in-
voked by Poe: *Omne tulit punctum, qui miscuit utile dulci;*
we reorganized the magazine and established an editorial
procedure; and we refurnished and redecorated the *Lit* offices.
One of the features of this latter transformation was a large
wooden settle, painted black, in the back of which we sawed
diamond-shaped holes and which we set against the long
front windows in such a way that we were screened from the
campus but able to watch all that went on there—a device
which we regarded as at once a symbol and a facilitation of
the semi-godlike role of the critic. These activities of ours,
of course—though we were not at first aware of it—were
reflecting and were a part of the general revival in literary
activity which was going on all through the United States,
and they were paralleled in the other colleges. We amused
ourselves by sending one day for two little volumes of verse
which had been printed by the author himself in Rutherford,
New Jersey, and which had been advertised in the local
paper. We had a library of bad poetry in the *Lit* office, and
we hoped they would turn out to be funny; but we were

puzzled by what we got. The poems *were* some of them quite funny, regarded from the conventional point of view; but they had also a kind of spare dignity, and were they wholly without merit? The poet was William Carlos Williams. A volume of plays called *Thirst* which reached us in 1914 was reviewed in the *Lit* as follows: "This volume, by Eugene G. O'Neill, contains five one-act plays which, if it were not for the author's manifest intention of making them something else, we should call very trashy . . ."

I had begun to have hopes of our producing some first-rate writers. It was true that the only contemporaries (Henry James was already a classic) that I could read with any genuine enthusiasm were Edith Wharton and E. A. Robinson; but the year before I came to college I had discovered H. L. Mencken, and I could see that there were possibilities for a kind of American literature which would not necessarily be published, as Mrs. Wharton and Robinson were, under the auspices of W. C. Brownell, at that time chief editor at Scribner's. Mr. Brownell, as I was afterwards to learn, was rejecting at that very moment—admitting that it was very able but protesting that it was impossible for Scribner's—Van Wyck Brooks's important book, *America's Coming-of-Age,* which handled our national classics rather impatiently and called for something better. But between our generation and the Civil War there had extended a kind of weedy or arid waste where people with an appreciation of literature had hardly hoped to find anything of value growing and where they had tended to be suspicious of anything that did manage to bloom; and T. K., a few years older than I, had grown up with the outlook of this period. Not only was there no interest at that time in the conventional academic world in anything that Americans were doing or might do; there was not even any real interest in our classics. I remember my surprise at first hearing that Professor Lounsbury of Yale occupied himself with American subjects. At Princeton Duncan Spaeth was a permanent scandal by reason of his admiration for Whitman: "Born on Long Island, died in Camden—found life beautiful!" Dr. Spaeth used to roar in defiance of people who, living close to Camden, assumed that it was too far away from the localities mentioned in *The Scholar Gypsy* to inspire the right kind of poetry. Thus, though T. K. read Mencken, too, with evident appetite, he used to confront me with incomprehension when I talked to him about working our own field. "You mean," he said to me one day at the Graduate School, when I was telling him that I'd rather stay at home than do as James and the rest had done, "that you'd rather be a big toad in a small puddle?"

I believe that those years at the Graduate School were, apart from his interest in the *Lit,* rather a barren time for T. K. I think of him always as enmeshed in two interminable Ph.D. theses: one on the influence of the Greek orator Isocrates on Milton's prose style, the other on the seventeenth-century epigram. There was something rather nightmarish about it: at first there had been only one thesis which he was

never able to finish, and then presently there were two, and
I felt that the whole thing was hopeless. I used to go over to
see him in the Graduate School, a sumptuous Gothic creation
which had just been erected by Ralph Adams Cram in the
middle of the Princeton golf links and which was then being
broken in. T. K. would invite me to a dreary enough dinner
in the immense medieval dining hall, where the faculty sat
on a daïs and the students filed in in black gowns to the
boom of a fugue of Bach from a hand-carved organ loft. The
Graduate School was a luxurious affair, and there was something about that life he liked. But, as a man from Kansas
City, he couldn't help being funny about the suits of armor
in the halls; and I never went over to see him without a feeling of desolation. I would traverse the enclosed court, where
the new gray stone in its rawness did not in the least remind
you of the stone of Oxford or Cambridge. I would ascend the
monastic stair, knock at the oaken door, and find T. K. inert
in his Morris chair, imprisoned amid the leaded windows,
unable to bring himself to get through any more volumes of
seventeenth-century epigrams and unwilling or without any
appetite to read anything more attractive. It was as if he had
succumbed to some terrible doom from which he was power-
less to save himself and from which nobody else could save
him. The whole spectacle gave me a horror of Ph.D. theses
from which I have never recovered.

Then the War reached America, and the board of the *Lit*
were dispersed. T. K. somehow managed to finish his thesis

and get his Ph.D. degree, and enlisted in the Marines and
went to France. There he came down with sarcoma of the
bladder and spent many miserable months in hospital. After
the War, he taught English for a time at Union College,
Schenectady—a town of which he wrote me that the inhabitants were "devoid of the attractive qualities alike of men
and of animals."

I felt even more depressed about him than I had when
he was studying at the Graduate School, so that I was very
much surprised and cheered when I suddenly found him
emerging in an entirely new role. I began to come upon
articles by him on contemporary American subjects—articles
of a quality which set them apart from anything else of the
kind being done; and when I would see him on his rare trips
to New York I would find him full of something more than
even his old enthusiasm of the *Lit* days about what was being
written in America. In 1928 he published a volume called
Spokesmen, which contained essays on Henry Adams, E. A.
Robinson, Dreiser, Frost, Anderson, Cather, Sandburg, Lindsay, Lewis, and O'Neill—the whole literary world of the
'twenties, in which I did not know he had been interested.
He said in his foreword that Van Wyck Brooks had "first
awakened" in him "the desire to try to understand the United
States." There was no ballyhoo in *Spokesmen;* there was not
even the patriotic leniency that lets its subjects off from dam-
aging questions and comparisons; but there was the definite

recognition that a new cultural era had opened. "Americans," he wrote, "for the first time in their history are seeking honest self-knowledge instead of self-glorification. The nation is self-conscious, with an eager curiosity as to all that concerns itself past or present, with a genuine desire to get acquainted with itself. It is willing to be told bitter truth, so long as it is told something about itself. If anyone is skeptical as to the awakening in the United States, I invite him to revert in his mind to the year 1910 or thereabouts, and ask himself whether the United States is not more alive now than then. ... All over the United States there is a stirring and a striving—after no one knows what. But the new life has already by its achievements established a claim to respect. It has produced buildings and books and plays and pictures which entitle it to admiration."

In the meantime he had gone to teach at Berkeley, where his courses became extremely popular. He had sometimes a nostalgia for Princeton, and he used to complain of the vacuity of California; but he found there an eager audience and security in his academic position, and he seems to have felt behind him the life of the whole country as I had never known him to do in the East. His field was lying right there before him, though he hadn't been able to see it from the Princeton Graduate School, and as soon as he began to work it, it was plain that this was the thing he should do. The Middle Westerner in T. K. came forward to meet the Middle Western writers who were playing such a conspicuous part

in the American literature of the period; but he met them
with the cultivated intelligence which was supposed to be
characteristic of the East. He was, I think, the first of our
critics to study the new novelists and dramatists and poets
at the same time appreciatively and calmly, to try to see the
work of each as a whole and to sum it up so far as it had
gone. Mencken and Rascoe and the rest had made people
read the new writers; and now the process of understanding them and appraising them was beginning with T. K.
Whipple.

These essays of T. K.'s, to one who had known him, were
a special cause of satisfaction. When one is ten years out of
college, one has already seen so many gifted friends fail to
do any of the things one had hoped of them, and it was
stimulating to find a man who had never made pretensions
or been petted accomplishing something excellent. His writing had certain characteristics excessively rare in the 'twenties: he knew precisely what he wanted to say, and he said
it with equanimity. He somehow—what seems to me unique
among the men of my acquaintance of our generation—got
through not only the 'twenties but even the 'thirties without
being thrown off his base. The good sense and good taste
which had distinguished him at college in the placid days
before the War somehow survived all those years when other
people were going to pieces and finding themselves bent
into unexpected shapes. I had felt in him already at college
a stoicism, a kind of resignation, which was not at all char-

acteristic of the American undergraduate. I had been struck
by his quoting to me from *Rasselas,* seriously and not merely
for the phrase, the characterization of human life as a state
(I may not have it quite right) "where much is to be suffered
and little known." Now the malady which had disabled him
in the army was menacing him with painful recurrences
through the remaining twenty years of his life; and it may be
that a conscious or unconscious awareness of the fate that was
always following him contributed to make him indifferent
to many things through which others became demoralized.

It was all the more remarkable, then, that a new social-
political interest should have begun to show itself in his work.
I was surprised again in the 'thirties at the force of the demo-
cratic instincts which were stirred by the literature of the
Left and which caused him to declare himself a socialist.
This was a common enough phenomenon at that period, but
it was not common to find criticism from the Left so un-
hysterical and unstampeded as Whipple's. As will be seen
from the essays in this book, the fine discriminations and
pressures of his mind managed to digest even a considerable
dose of Marxism without absorbing from it anything but
nourishment; and looking back on his career at college, with
its emphases that were so quiet yet so definite, his attitude
toward the eating-club system and his policy with contributors to the *Lit,* I could see that these equalitarian instincts
did not now get out of hand because they had always been
there. I imagine that his experience of the War, in which he

had served without a commission, had wakened, as it did in most such cases, a sympathy with the common man which remained with him ever after. He had shared the solidarity of the Marine Corps, and he always felt the special pride in it which is characteristic of that branch of the service.

He responded at any rate to the times with a liveliness and youthfulness that were amazing—though I have found that those men and women who really live in close contact with the arts remain young when the people who live with the ups and downs of business, of the stock market, or of current politics, become stale with middle age. I last saw him in 1938 when he had got a sabbatical year from Berkeley and come East to write a new book. He could hardly have been fuller of projects if he had just got out of college. He had come out to see me in the country, and it was quite like the old *Nassau Lit* days when he had used to drop over from the Graduate School. But now he no longer had to think about Isocrates. He was going to write about things that excited him and about which he had something to say, and he knew that there were people who would read him.

He died suddenly of a recurrence of his malady in the spring of the following year (June 3, 1939); but the pieces included in this volume, which were to be part of the material for his book, show how the glow of that light which had survived days of dullness and days of pain was intensified to a special brightness just before it went out.

December, 1942

Study Out the Land

Machinery, Magic, and Art

MOST PEOPLE seem to feel, vaguely and perhaps uncomfortably, that the arts somehow ought to be thought of as important. We permit our children in school to give their time to music and drawing. Our self-made men often devote part of their hard-won earnings to paintings or old books. As soon as our cities accumulate a little spare capital, they start public libraries and orchestras and art galleries. Nevertheless, the lot of the arts is not an altogether happy one. The practitioner of any art is apt to feel that the homage paid the arts is largely sham, and that he is in reality surrounded by a vast ocean of indifference and incomprehension. He and his cohorts are inclined to take to scolding the public or the nation. And the public, on the other hand, when at intervals it is seized with compunction and decides to investigate what is happening in the arts, is likely to find itself puzzled and vexed, and forced to the conclusion that the modern painter or musician or poet "only does it to annoy." It gladly returns to its old favorites, or to its old unconcern.

Meanwhile, becalmed upon this windless sea of neglect, the artists and their hangers-on degenerate into connoisseurs and virtuosos and technicians, and quarrel over the functions and purposes of their several arts, and lament the crassness of

the modern age. Yet the responsibility for the present unsatis-
factory state of affairs must be charged chiefly to the artists.
The modern age—for all the disparagement of it which we
hear from those who do not belong to it in spirit—is as good
as another, if not better. And the public is on the whole
right—right in its sense both that the arts ought to be important, and that they somehow aren't. Surely, everyone has a
drastic, vital need of art—for reasons which I shall try to set
forth later on. And for a long time now the arts have done
little to fill this need.

In the theoretical discussions which rage among the spe-
cialists, many purposes are propounded—and these, it is true,
the arts fulfill: they give much pleasure, they afford self-
expression to many, they supply a representation, an interpretation, a criticism of life. At their best, they do what Robert
Frost says art should do—"strip life to form." Yet the fact
remains that nowadays painting and music and literature are
luxury products.

To turn to the one art that really flourishes in our time—
engineering, and especially mechanical engineering—is in-
structive. The fact that this is not a fine art, but a utilitarian
one, long prevented it from being recognized as an art at all.
However, the presupposition that nothing useful can be art,
a notion general among both the aesthetic clans and the laity,
is directly opposite to the truth, and has wrought great harm.
On the contrary, there ought to be no fine arts, but only useful ones. And mechanical engineering has prospered because

there is no doubt as to what it accomplishes, and because that is something everybody wants done: it transmits and regulates power, and everyone wants command of power, ever more power. Thus, this one art that thrives has two lessons to teach the fine arts: that any art can flourish if it will satisfy a strong universal desire; and that what men crave is power. In other words, I suggest that artists set themselves the same end as mechanicians—the communication and control of power. This is the all-important function which modern art has abandoned.

Of late there has been some talk, and very interesting talk, too, about machines as works of art. Why not reverse the process, and look at works of art as machines? Such an identification of art and machinery is not unwarranted. In the beginning they were one and the same thing, they served the same single object, the gaining and ruling of power. This was in the days when they were both indistinguishable parts of primitive magic. As they have developed and differentiated, however, machinery has remained true to its original purpose, but specialized in handling only physical power. Art, on the other hand, which should specialize in conveying psychological power, has relinquished its office. Consequently, it finds itself in the doldrums, although it has vital work to do that can be done by no other agency. The world has urgent need of it; both the world and art would benefit if the arts could be persuaded to resume their original and proper business, to play once again the role they played in early magic.

The mention of magic ought not to be too surprising. It
has long been recognized that in primitive magic lies a chief
source of both science and art. Magic is the savage's engineering, his technology. It is his effort to get command of power
and direct it to his own purposes. By mimicry, incantation,
and the other methods of magic he undertakes to control the
wind and the rains, to induce fecundity in his tribe, to make
his crops grow. Always he has in view, according to his lights,
what Bacon foretold as the chief service of natural science,
"the relief of man's estate." And it must be remembered that
to him magic is in a sense not magic, and certainly not to be
divided from science and art. To divert the waters of a stream
to his cornfield, to sprinkle it with holy meal, and to make
a song or a statue for the benefit of his grain are for him not
only equally valid but similar means of attaining his end.

Furthermore, it must be remembered also that, not dis-
criminating as we do between objective and subjective, he
sees physical and psychological energy as all one. He con-
ceives of a universal potency in which all things share to a
greater or lesser degree; the terms of the Maori and of the
Sioux for this potency, *mana* and *wakanda* respectively, have
come into wide use among anthropologists. The common
American word is "medicine." Just as we wish above everything to get at what we call energy and use it for ourselves,
so the savage wishes to avail himself of what he calls *mana*—
the two words mean much the same thing. From the individual's private relations with the Powers Above and Below

to the communal rites of the whole tribe runs the same motive, the winning and directing of power.

After all, the ways of the savage are not so utterly different
from our own. In time of war, for instance, as we invent new
explosives and machine guns, he makes himself the best bows
and arrows that he can. His fighters do their war dances;
our soldiers march and sing. He paints the Thunderbird and
other mighty spirits on his equipment to get their assistance;
we try to reassure ourselves in our churches that Omnipotence
is with us. It is curious to reflect how many of our devices for
keeping up our morale, or for sustaining our tribal *wakanda,*
are like those of the savage—that is, are magical. And very
effective these devices are, too, as everybody knows.

For unquestionably there is truth in magic, as well as de-
lusion—but it is psychological, not scientific truth. The love
song or the war song, the amulet in which he has faith, beyond doubt render a man more irresistible in love or war, if
only by heartening him. By similar means, it is probable,
medicine men have succeeded in curing many illnesses. In
the fertility rites of spring, we may question the efficacy of
the ceremony with reference to the crops, but we have no
reason to question its efficacy with reference to the tribe itself.
In relation to external objects, we know that magic fails; but
we ought to know also that with reference to the practitioners
themselves it is likely to succeed: by means of it they gain an
access of energy—they gain the power they desire.

No one, I am sure, who has ever witnessed a genuine mag-

ical ceremony will question its effectiveness. In January a
year ago I happened to see the animal dance or hunting dance
at the pueblo of Jemez in New Mexico. At dawn a band of
men, singers and drummers, go forth to the hills and call in
the animals—that is, men wearing the skins of buffalo, deer,
antelope, and the like. Then, hour after hour, the rite pro-
ceeds in the plaza of the pueblo, repeated again and again.
The band of men station themselves at the foot of the plaza,
and rising and falling chant and throbbing drums summon
forth the animals from the kiva, the ceremonial chamber
at the head of the plaza. Reluctantly the animals come out,
and, resisting every step, and with many efforts to escape,
are slowly drawn by the pull of the chant. When they reach
the drums, the music breaks into a wild climax, and the men
drive the animals step by step up the plaza and back into the
kiva. Then the process begins anew.

The ostensible purpose is plainly to secure success in hunting, by first calling the game out and then driving it in. Thus
the tribe should get dominion over its prey, and bring home
much meat during the season. But these Indians have not
been hunters for many years. The function which the rite
actually performs is quite different. I should say that it is a
heightening of the physical vitality and vigor of the tribe, an
increase in animal energy. Even the ignorant and infidel by-
stander gains from it a tremendous lift, a renewal, and an
enhancement of strength. After all, we have our bodies, we
are part animal, and to get a proper relation to our bodily

animal energies, instincts, powers—the groundwork of our lives—is of enormous benefit. The Indians, in present conditions, need these things more than ever before, and therefore, though no longer hunters, they still profit from performing their magic rite.

Magic, then, so far as it is efficacious and true, might be described as a kind of psychological machinery—that is, a set of devices by which the human being is enabled to avail himself of augmented psychological power, to raise his vitality. "Psychic energy," to be sure, may be only a metaphor, a figure of speech which we use to cover our ignorance, because we know too little to speak literally and exactly. Indeed, we might as well use the primitive terms, and call it *mana, wakanda,* "medicine," mysterious potency. But the phenomenon itself, in some form or other, I am sure, is familiar to everyone; everyone, that is, must be conscious at times of possessing a peculiar abundance of vigor, and at other times of its dearth. We have various methods of securing this vigor; the primitive secures it by the practice of magic.

Among the means by which magic works, the two most important, I suspect, are *images* and *rhythm.* The savage sings, he dances, he beats his drum—magical practices are replete with rhythmical activities. And rhythmical activity, as we all know from our own experience, sets free our latent energies. Probably it affects our breathing, the beating of our hearts, and the other bodily processes which are themselves rhythmical, speeding them up or toning them down, height-

ening them and making them more regular. At any rate,
whatever the cause, the effect of rhythm is familiar enough,
from the savage's war dance to the congregational singing in
church and to modern dancing.

As for images, their potency is perhaps less generally recognized. But consider the part played by images in magical
procedure—in the typical case, for instance, of the warrior's
magic, whether individual or communal. First of all, he holds
before his mind an image of success, of victory; he pictures
himself irresistibly slaying huge numbers of the enemy. Thus
he gains confidence, and therefore power. Furthermore, he
imagines himself receiving aid from nature; he keeps in his
mind an image of Wind or Sun, thus associating and identifying himself with forces mightier than his own. So his
own little "medicine" is enlarged by drawing upon the great
"medicines" of the world, and he is bucked up, he feels that
"virtue" has entered into him. A war song of the Blackfeet,
rendered by Miss Eda Lou Walton, illustrates the process:

> The earth is my home,
> It is powerful.
> Water speaks in foam,
> It is powerful.
> There sits a hill,
> It is powerful.
> I go now to kill,
> I am powerful!

Strong as the image in the mind may be, however, its
strength is immensely increased if it is embodied in some-

thing, and so objectified and externalized. The mere association of it with some external object seems to be of much help:
the possession of a wolf's tooth or an eagle's feather, for example, aids in addressing prayer for ferocity or speed to the
Wolf or Eagle Spirit—aids presumably by making more vivid
and real the image involved. Still more effective is a drawing,
a picture, a carving of wood or stone—any such representation
of the Power to be won. This is the "image" in the sense of
effigy or likeness, as in the Biblical phrase "graven image."
It is noteworthy that no religion has been able to get along
without such images for long—a testimonial to the inability
of most people to hold a mental image without help, and to
the superior efficacy of the objective image. To the methods
of achieving this result should be added the embodying of
an image in the mimicry and movements of a dance, and the
snaring of it in the words and music of a song. These last
methods are of special consequence, because they unite strik-
ingly the two most effectual of the instruments of magic,
both rhythm and image.

According to the civilized view, the savage, in the act of
creating his charm, whether fetish or song or dance, frees and
utilizes latent energy in himself; and thereafter the charm
has the capacity at proper moments again to make latent
energy available, through working upon him with imagery
and rhythm. But this of course is not at all the savage's view.
He believes that the charm itself possesses the *mana;* and he
further believes that once the charm is made, its *mana* be-

comes transferable. The original owner and maker, by giving his talisman to someone else, or by teaching his song or his dance to another, can pass on with it its "medicine." Thus, a man, for instance, who makes a good hunting dance or song may be thought a great benefactor to his tribe. And quite properly, too, for these charms do no doubt produce much the same psychological effect upon others as upon the creators of them. So the man who devises a good war dance may make better fighters of all his clansmen, by enhancing their belligerent ardor.

It must be clear by this time what a large part magic has played in the origin of the arts. Other sources also may have contributed: probably wood was carved and pictures drawn for the mere fun of it; probably from the beginning some songs were sheer outbursts of spontaneous feeling. But serious art, art that mattered, was pretty well tied up with magic; a work of art was a magical machine, a contrivance for capturing *mana,* potency. Songs and dances were spells, charms; rituals and pantomimes developed into drama and opera and choral singing; modern fiction is related to the ceremonial rehearsing of sacred myths; and painting and sculpture began mainly in primitive fetishes and idols. Bach and Beethoven are lineal descendants of early shamans and medicine men. Art as well as science has grown out of the basic impulse which underlies magic. But whereas science, at least applied science, has remained true to its first aim, the arts, in our world, have drifted far away.

That is my complaint of them. In surrendering their practical usefulness, they have relinquished their chief excuse for being. And only, I venture to say, when they return to their first function, when they become again channels of power, will they regain the robust vitality and the wide acceptance and understanding which they have forfeited. For everyone craves more vital energy, more medicine or *wakanda,* and when artists supply it they will no longer have cause to complain of public indifference. The triumphs and services of science and engineering are not more momentous, I venture to say, in utilizing natural resources, than might be the triumphs and services of art in utilizing human resources.

All art that amounts to much has been true to its original function, and has attained its end by magical means: by rhythm and images—embodied, externalized images. The Greek tragedies were not performed, nor the Gothic cathedrals built, we may be sure, merely to gratify the aesthetic sense, but to do something, to perform work on the beholders. Later artists, too, have been conscious of this aspect of their work. When Browning describes the effect on a band of pirates of listening to poetry, he says:

> And then, because Greeks are Greeks,
> And hearts are hearts, and *poetry is power,*
> They all outbrake in a great joyous laughter
> With much love.

The effect of, say, imagist verse on bands of Americans is very different from that. And before deciding that Americans

are insensitive, let us ask, "Is this poetry power?" Of all qualities demanded of poetry nowadays, we hear least of this, that
it communicate power. And most of the poets, too, seem to
have forgotten this purpose. But Browning was well aware
of it, as witness his *Saul,* in which David by singing wins
Saul back from death to life, and in which Browning himself
exemplifies the fact that poetry can be power, can be charged
and surcharged with tremendous "medicine."

From the artist's point of view, Byron has said the last
word: as the artist gives shape and body to his imaginings,
he gets back from them the vitality he imparts, and thus
increases the life that is in him:

> 'Tis to create, and in creating live
> A being more intense, that we endow
> With form our fancy, gaining as we give
> The life we image.

The artist expends much energy, but somehow he gets back
more. This is the magical and mysterious effect of artistic
creation. It is as if the images, hidden in his mind, contained
great stores of energy, but locked up, latent, inert, which are
set free and made available. To take a conspicuous example
of figures which have the kind of power in question, think
of Michelangelo's "Night" or his "Adam": these figures, we
may suppose, lay secretly in Michelangelo's mind, unknown
to himself, rich in inactive power; then, as they rose before his
mind at the moment of conception, and still more, vastly
more, as he projected them in marble and in paint, this power

was liberated and flooded his consciousness, so that, in Byron's words, he gained, as he gave it, the life he imaged, and lived "a being more intense." In other words, we may be sure that "Night" or "Adam" had for Michelangelo the value that his fetish or his charm has for a savage—an embodiment and a source of supernal energy, of *wakanda,* of mysterious potency. Just as the primitive carves or paints or sings to get at this potency, so does the artist.

And just as the charm, together with its power, is transferable, so also—luckily for most of us—is the work of art. It is as if a great musical composition or building or play were an inexhaustible reservoir or store of energy. It transmits to us the power which its creator poured into it. Upon it we can draw for a heightening of vitality, for more abundant life. Nor should it be assumed that only the stately and sublime works of art possess this quality; on the contrary, much popular art has it, and indeed I question whether any art or artist that altogether lacks it can be widely popular. For example, I should say that *The Big Parade* and Charlie Chaplin and Fanny Brice and *Old Man River* and Zane Grey all had more or less of it. Perhaps indeed at present the lowbrow arts have more of it than the highbrow. But at any time people will flock to the artist who will move them, do something to them—who will give them that enhancement of life which we all crave. We care so much for it that we will even suffer to get it—and this, I am sure, is why we enjoy tragic art. In spite of the pain involved, the tragic spectacle exalts our own sense of life; it transmits to us the artist's passion and energy, and so gives us a lift, an augmented vitality. Freudians, and others before them, have maintained that all art, and tragedy in particular, are of service chiefly in cleansing bosoms of perilous stuff. But surely art's function is less important as a purgative or a safety valve than as an unbounded source of energy.

I have suggested that art works upon us as magic works upon the savage—by rhythm, and by embodied images. But I think the effect of art is more understandable if for *rhythm* the larger term *order* or *harmony* is substituted. If a poem, a statue, or a building is patterned or ordered in a form, as it should be, if it is a harmonious embodiment of power, it conveys that power to us in order and harmony, and so induces a corresponding harmony in ourselves. Now most of us are seldom in a wholly harmonious state; most of the time much of our energy is absorbed and wasted in strains and conflicts, outer and inner; we do not often, so to speak, hit on all cylinders. Therefore, to be harmonized is for us to be energized— to be "put in order," literally, is to experience an increase of power. This is why *form* is all-important in art; it corresponds to efficiency in a machine; the power involved, instead of being lost, is communicated so as to do the work it ought to do.

If the form makes it possible for the power to be transmitted, the carrier of that power is the image. The importance of imagination is grossly underestimated today, probably because for various reasons modern life is marked by an exaggerated objectivity. But for all our externality, our running away from ourselves into outer circumstances and hectic activity, our lives are still largely ruled by images. We imagine ourselves wealthy, or powerful, or learned, or famous, or irresistible in love, or having exciting adventures, and we set ourselves to acquire what we have imagined. Many men and women, possessed by imagination, have cast themselves for roles beyond their capacities, and striven to be superhuman heroes or saints or sages. For weal or woe, images have dominion over us, and it is of the utmost consequence that we be aware of them, conscious of what is happening; that we be not obsessed by them, but judge their fitness for ourselves and our situation. And art, by embodying them in some external medium, helps us to this awareness, enables us to avoid obsession, to distinguish between ourselves and these images. It does not shear them of their power, but it changes that power from obsessive to beneficial.

Miss Rebecca West's phrase, "the potent image," is a good one. I have not meant to imply that any or every image is potent; most of them are not. One may imagine oneself walking downstairs or washing one's face, but the image has no special value for oneself or anyone else. And only potent images have value for art. The most valuable are those which are racial or national, or, still better, universal. The figure of Don Quixote has been of enormous worth to Spain; the figure of Robin Hood has had a particular attraction for English-

men. Perhaps the nearest that America has come to such
"potent images" is in Lincoln or Jesse James—the mythical,
not the historical figures—or in the Indian. The viking ap-
peals to all northern races. Such figures as Prometheus the
Fire-bringer, or Faust, the man who sold himself to the devil,
have a world-wide significance. The potent image, however,
need not be human, nor even naturalistic. Oddly enough, it
may even be mathematical. The embodiments in architecture
and in music of abstract imagination, of pure form, can be
as moving as any. There is no way, so far as I know, of telling
which images will have potency and which will not—but the
quality itself is unmistakable.

Sometimes it looks as if modern artists by preference busied
themselves with impotent images. They seem to avoid images which profoundly move themselves or anyone else, to
be distrustful of imagination and above all of emotion. And
they have their reward, in comparative neglect and misun-
derstanding. The public cannot be expected to comprehend,
much less to care violently about, subtle problems of technique. But meanwhile, unfortunately, the public suffers even
more than the artists from this state of affairs. To be sure,
there is all the art of the past to draw upon, but somehow
with the lapse of time works of art suffer a gradual loss of
power. By no means a total loss, of course, or we should be
hard put to it; but it would be absurd to suppose that the
Bacchae of Euripides or *Le Misanthrope* of Molière can mean
as much to us as to their original audiences. The images which

were potent in ancient Greece or under the Ancien Régime
are naturally much less potent in the twentieth-century
United States.

For these reasons, if we are to get the power which only
art can give us, we must have artists of our own to convey it.
And we are not without them. There is little ground to complain of our architects. Some of our writers perform their
function. Musicians seem less satisfactory; and few sculptors
or painters in the United States aim at transmitting power.
Just now, this function has been largely relegated to the
cheapest practitioners—in literature, for instance, to Zane
Grey and Edgar Rice Burroughs. However, there is no reason
to suppose that the public prefers inadequate and incompetent art. O'Neill has not lacked his audiences, and even a
poem—witness *John Brown's Body*—if it will do its job, can
attract hordes of readers. But the public in its demands has
been faithful to the original purpose of art; it asks magic and
power, and if good artists deny it, it turns to bad ones.

The result is deplorable all round. While the artists take
for their motto, "No compromise with the public taste," and
wither away in minute elaboration of their individual, private, and insignificant moods and sensations and skills, the
public feeds on husks and straw. Yet I cannot believe that our
artists are incapable of conceiving powerful forms and images
of more than personal significance, which would profoundly
stir them, and therefore us too. I believe rather that, mis-
apprehending their function, they do not solicit such forms

and images. For too long they have thought of themselves as playing no social role. It is as if a savage, instead of using his magic for the major purposes of living, were to use it only for private entertainment; as if a mechanical engineer, instead of helping get the world's work done, were to design only toys to amuse himself. We need the artists, as we need imperatively the kind of life and power which only they can supply. Let us beg them not to desert us utterly.

[1931]

American Sagas

As everyone knows, the latest fad of the intelligentsia is discovering the United States. This is the cult of which Mr. Gilbert Seldes is high priest. He and his acolytes wax analytic and aesthetic over Charlie Chaplin, Fanny Brice, Krazy Kat, Ring Lardner, and "How Come You Do Me Like You Do Do Do." And, indeed, why not? The rest of us may be amused at the delighted surprise with which recent graduates of Harvard "discover" what everyone else has been familiar with since earliest childhood—but the fact remains that Mr. Seldes has secured for our popular arts a recognition that they never had before. Already jazz has invaded Carnegie Hall, and before long everyone may be attending recitals not of Lithuanian, Swedish, and Bantu folk songs only, but of American as well. The Negro spirituals have arrived; why not the ballads of cowboys, lumberjacks, and Kentucky mountaineers?

While the boom is on, I wish to put in a word for the tales of the American folk. In Paris, according to hearsay, one of the more recent literary finds is James Oliver Curwood, whose art is discussed at length in periodicals and reviews. My own nominee, however, for the position of American *tusitala* is not Mr. Curwood, but Zane Grey. Mr. Grey has received justice only from his millions of devoted readers—

and some of them, I fear, have been shamefaced in their enthusiasm. The critics and reviewers have been persistently
upstage in their treatment of Mr. Grey; they have lectured
him for lacking qualities which there was no reason for him
to possess, and have ignored most of the qualities in which
he is conspicuous. The Boston *Transcript* complains that "he
does not ask his readers to think for themselves"; Mr. Burton
Rascoe asks sorrowfully: "Do Mr. Grey's readers believe in
the existence of such people as Mr. Grey depicts; do they
accept the code of conduct implicit in Mr. Grey's novels?"

One thing at least is clear: Mr. Grey himself emphatically
believes in the truthfulness of his record. Above all else he
prides himself upon his accuracy as a historian. In the foreword to *To the Last Man* he says: "My long labors have been
devoted to making stories resemble the times they depict. I
have loved the West for its vastness, its contrast, its beauty
and color and life, for its wildness and violence, and for the
fact that I have seen how it developed great men and women
who died unknown and unsung." And he asks: "How can
the truth be told about the pioneering of the West if the
struggle, the fight, the blood be left out? How can a novel
be stirring and thrilling, as were those times, unless it be
full of sensation?" One must admire and be thankful for
Mr. Grey's faith in his own veracity; but to share it is impossible. Zane Grey should never be considered as a realist.
To Mr. Rascoe's questions, I can answer for only one reader,
but I should say that I no more believe in the existence of

such people as Mr. Grey's than I believe in the existence of
the shepherds of Theocritus; I no more accept the code of
conduct implicit in Mr. Grey's novels than I do the code of
conduct implicit in Congreve's comedies. At the very start
I grant that Mr. Grey does not portray the world as I know
it, that he is not an expert psychologist, that his is no refined
art in the subtle use of words—that in competition with
Henry James, Jane Austen, George Eliot, and Laurence
Sterne he is nowhere.

But what of it? There is no reason for comparing him with
anyone, unless perhaps with competitors in his own genre.
If he must be classified, however, let it be with the authors
of *Beowulf* and of the Icelandic sagas. Mr. Grey's work is a
primitive epic, and has the characteristics of other primitive
epics. His art is archaic, with the traits of all archaic art. His
style, for example, has the stiffness which comes from an imperfect mastery of the medium. It lacks fluency and facility;
behind it always we feel a pressure toward expression, a striving for a freer and easier utterance. Herein lies much of the
charm of all early art—in that the technique lags somewhat
behind the impulse. On the whole, it is preferable to the
later condition, when the technique is matured and the impulse meager. Mr. Grey's style has also the stiffness of traditional and conventional forms; his writing is encrusted
with set phrases which may be called epic formulae, or, if you
insist, clichés. These familiar locutions he uses as if they were
new, to him at least—as if they were happy discoveries of his

own. So behind all his impeded utterance there makes itself felt an effort toward truth of expression—truth, that is, to his own vision, for we must never ask of him truth to the actual world as we know it.

That Zane Grey has narrative power no one has denied, but not everyone is pleased with his type of story. To a reader whose taste has been formed on Howells and Bennett, Mr. Grey's tales seem somewhat strong. They are, of course, sensational melodrama, as "improbable" as plays by Elizabethan dramatists. They roar along over the mightiest stage that the author has been able to contrive for them. They tell of battle and bloodshed, of desperate pursuits and hairbreadth escapes, of mortal feuds and murder and sudden death, of adventures in which life is constantly the stake. These stories move on the grand scale; they are lavish in primitive, epic events. Mr. Grey does not dodge big scenes and crises, in which plot and passion come to a head; he has a distinct liking for intense situations, and he has the power which Stevenson so admired of projecting these high moments in memorable pictures. In *Riders of the Purple Sage,* when Lassiter throws his guns on the Mormon band and saves the Gentile youth, when Venters from his hiding place in the mysterious canyon watches the robbers ride through the waterfall, when at last Lassiter rolls the stone which crushes his pursuers and forever shuts the outlet from Surprise Valley—these are scenes which linger in the mind. Very different, obviously, is this art from Mrs. Wharton's when she condenses the tragedy of three

lives into the breaking of a pickle dish, and from Sinclair
Lewis' as he takes Babbitt through a typical day at the office.
But what of that? Though melodrama is not in style at the
moment, the human taste for tremendous happenings is not
likely to die for some centuries yet. Mr. Grey has the courage
of his innocence in tackling difficulties which cautious real-
ists know enough to avoid.

And no more than in his stories does he dodge the heroic
in his characters. His people are all larger than life size. They
may be called cowpunchers, prospectors, ranchers, rangers,
rustlers, highwaymen, but they are akin to Sigurd, Beowulf,
and Robin Hood. Just at present, heroism, of all literary mo-
tifs, happens to be the most unfashionable, and disillusionment is all the cry. But it is tenable surely that the heroic is
not incompatible with literary merit, and perhaps even that
a naïve belief in human greatness is a positive asset to literature. Certainly of the writings in the past which humanity
has singled out for special favor most have this element,
notoriously strong in all early literature.

Of these heroic figures Mr. Grey's portrayal is crude and
roughhewn. Their speech is often far from the talk of actual
men and women; we are as much—and as little—conscious
of the writer's working in a literary convention as when we
read a play in blank verse. His characterization has no subtlety or finesse; but, like his style, it is true—again, of course,
I mean true to the author's own conception. That conception
of human nature is a simple one; he sees it as a battle of pas-

sions with one another and with the will, a struggle of love
and hate, of remorse and revenge, of blood lust, honor, friend-
ship, anger, grief—all on a grand scale and all incalculable
and mysterious. The people themselves are amazed and incredulous at what they find in their own souls. A good illus-
tration of Mr. Grey's psychological analysis is the following
from *The Lone Star Ranger:*

> Then came realization. . . . He was the gunman, the gun-thrower,
> the gun-fighter, passionate and terrible. His father's blood, that
> dark and fierce strain, his mother's spirit, that strong and unquench-
> able spirit of the surviving pioneer—these had been in him; and
> the killings, one after another, the wild and haunted years, had
> made him, absolutely in spite of his will, the gunman. He realized
> it now, bitterly, hopelessly. The thing he had intelligence enough
> to hate he had become. At last he shuddered under the driving,
> ruthless, inhuman blood-lust of the gunman.

In Zane Grey's conception of human nature nothing is
more curious than his view of sex. In *Riders of the Purple
Sage* a young man and a girl live alone together for weeks
in a secret canyon; in *The Lone Star Ranger* the hero rescues
an innocent girl from a gang of bandits and roams about
Texas with her for a long time—and all as harmlessly as in
The Faerie Queene Una and the Red Cross Knight go travel-
ing together. Nothing shows more clearly how far away Mr.
Grey's world is from actuality; his Texas is not in the Union,
but in fairyland. His heroes, to be sure, have occasional fierce
struggles with their "baser natures"—a difficulty, by the way,
from which his heroines are exempt. Not all his women,

however, are altogether pure; from time to time a seductress crosses the path of the hero, who usually regards her with indifference. These women, incidentally, are often among the best-drawn of Mr. Grey's characters. In his treatment of sex as in other respects Mr. Grey is simple and naïve; his conventions are as remote as those of the medieval Courts of Love, and must be taken for granted along with the other assumptions of his imaginary world.

Mr. Grey's heroic ideal looks a little strange in the twentieth century. It is; it belongs more naturally to the sixth century; it is the brutal ideal of the barbarian, of the Anglo-Saxons before they left their continental homes. Like them, Mr. Grey cares above all things for physical strength, for prowess in battle and expertness with weapons, for courage and fortitude and strength of will, for ability to control oneself and others. Where the Anglo-Saxon emphasized loyalty in thegn and generosity in earl, Mr. Grey more democratically insists on loyalty and generosity between friends, and on independence and self-reliance. And to this code he adds an element which is no doubt a kind of residuum from Christianity: he likes to see hatred and desire for vengeance supplanted by forgiveness and love. The process of purification or redemption is a favorite theme of his; sometimes it is brought about by the influence of a noble and unselfish man or by the love of a pure and innocent girl, but more often by the cleansing effect of nature in the rough. If one is to take Mr. Grey's ethics at all seriously, one must of course find fault with them; although such morals are better, no doubt, than those inculcated by Benjamin Franklin or Mr. Ben Hecht, still one would no more care to have one's sons adopt Mr. Grey's *beau idéal* than one would care to have one's sons adopt, say, the *Saga of Burnt Njal* as a program of life. Without wishing, however, to return to the human ideals of the Bronze Age, we may insist that a storyteller's merit is not dependent on the validity of the lessons which he teaches. There is something of the savage in most of us, so that we can respond imaginatively to Mr. Grey without our all rushing off to the wilds to be made men of.

Not that Mr. Grey regards nature as always a beneficent force. Rather, he portrays it as an acid test of those elemental traits of character which he admires. It kills off the weaklings, and among the strong it makes the bad worse and the good better. Nature to him is somewhat as God is to a Calvinist—ruthlessly favoring the elect and damning the damned. Mr. Grey sees in nature the great primal force which molds human lives. Not even Thomas Hardy lays more stress on the effect of natural environment. The stories themselves are subsidiary to the background: "My inspiration to write," says Mr. Grey, "has always come from nature. Character and action are subordinate to setting." This setting of desert, forest, mountain, and canyon, great cliffs and endless plains, has been made familiar to us all by the movies if not by travel; but as seen through Mr. Grey's marveling and enhancing eyes it all takes on a fresh and unreal greatness and wonder.

For his descriptive power is as generally recognized as his narrative skill; indeed, it would be hard for anyone so overflowing with zest and with almost religious adoration to fail in description. Mr. Grey's faculty of wonder, his sense of mystery, is strong; it shows itself in his feeling for the strangeness of human personality and also more outwardly in the air of strangeness with which he invests his lonely wanderers or outlaws who from time to time appear out of the unknown—but most of all it shows itself in his feeling for the marvelous in nature. So far as he indicates a religion, it is a form of nature worship; when he is face to face with the more grandiose aspects of the earth's surface, he feels himself in the presence of God.

Mr. Grey differs from many nature lovers, that is to say, in that his fervor is altogether genuine. His enthusiasm is not assumed because it is the proper thing; on the contrary, he feels much more than he can manage to express. And here, I think, we come to the secret of his superiority to most of his contemporaries and competitors: he is sincere and thoroughly in earnest. He really cares, he gets excited about what he is writing. His books have not the look of hackwork. It is true that they are uneven, that he has not been immune to the influences of his own popularity and of the movies, that he must often have worked hastily and carelessly—but he has never written falsely. He is genuine and true to himself, an artist after his fashion. Furthermore, he possesses a powerful imagination, of the mythmaking type which glorifies and enlarges all that it touches, and in his best work, such as *Riders of the Purple Sage,* he uses his imagination to the utmost. The whole story, the situations and people and settings, are fully living in his mind, and he gets them into words as best he can. Of course he has an amazing, an incredible simplicity and unsophistication of mind, a childlike naïveté—but that is what makes him what he is, a fashioner of heroic myths. At the present moment, when the primitive is all the vogue in the arts, and Viennese and Parisian sculptors are doing their best to be archaic, in Zane Grey we have a real, not a would-be, primitive miraculously dropped among us; yet we accord him no recognition at all—except an astounding popularity.

If, that is, his popularity is astounding—if it is not, rather, what should be expected. Most Americans seem to have a strongly ingrained hankering for the primitive and a good deal of the childlike quality of mind, possibly as an inheritance from our three centuries of pioneering. Whenever a holiday comes along, we reproduce primitive conditions and play at pioneering as much as possible. The age of the pioneers, especially in the West, is taking on more and more the air of a heroic and mythic period. The glorification of the redblooded he-man, the pioneer ideal, is a national trait, and even those who have learned better cannot rid themselves of a sneaking respect for the brute in their hearts. If you doubt the simplicity and innocence of Americans, watch their reactions to Michael Arlen and Jean Cocteau and their

forlorn efforts to imitate Ronald Firbank and to understand
and admire *Ulysses*. They are like stray Vandals wandering
bewildered through the streets of Byzantium. Only the pure
in heart could be so impressed by decay and corruption, just
as only a man from an Iowa village could have written *The
Blind Bow-Boy*. No, the American forte is not sophisticated
disillusion—it is much more likely to be something on the
order of Zane Grey's work. Of course everyone is at liberty
not to like such literature, which belongs by right to the
infancy of the race, and to disagree with Mr. Grey's view
of the world. Indeed, if one asks of books a valid criticism
of life as we experience it, Mr. Grey has little to offer. But let
us look at him for what he is, rather than what he is not.
Then, whether or not we happen to care for his work, I think
we must grant him a certain merit in his own way. We turn
to him not for insight into human nature and human problems nor for refinements of art, but simply for crude epic
stories, as we might to an old Norse skald, maker of the sagas
of the folk.

[1925]

The American Predicament

"HAS AMERICA ever been discovered?" asked the Englishman on board the westbound steamer, after someone had mentioned Columbus. Of course the only answer we could give him was "No." For it does not as yet even exist; it has not been created, or at best it is in process of creation. Only the eye of a prophet, and an omniscient prophet, could discover America. To be sure, many of the elements of which it will be made, and many of the forces which are molding it, are discoverable, but both elements and forces are discordant, numberless, incalculable, and the outcome is hidden in the dark of futurity.

Yet the American secret is easy to state: many people left old lands and came to live together in a new land. Only the implications of the statement give trouble. For one thing, the very term "old land" is an obstacle, to an American: he cannot truly understand its whole meaning. His imagination is unable to enter fully into the mind of a man whose forefathers and whose neighbors' forefathers have lived for a thousand years or more in the same locality. For thirty or fifty generations they have been seeing the same small fields, hedges, trees, in the morning and the evening the same lights and shadows, colors, clouds, and mists. They have heard the same birds sing—the skylark, the nightingale. They have pressed and drunk the same wine from the same grapes. Through nostril and ear and eye their surroundings have been working upon their brains.

Nor is the sensory impress the chief. More important is the identity of group life with place. All the experience of these people has been bound up with the particular soil on which they live—childhood, lovemaking, marriage, work and play. The harvest festival has been held, and the maypole set up in spring, time out of mind in some special spot. Their legends and superstitions tell how the ghost of so-and-so's ancestor walks under a certain thorn tree, how this or that well or spring is inhabited by a water spirit. For generations they have said their prayers at the wayside cross; their religion is colored by special veneration to the local saint, the local shrine. And their religion, their labor, their sport, all phases of their existence individual and communal, are mingled, fused, unified; every aspect of life is interwoven with every other—and all with the neighborhood.

Transport a man from such a community to a remote wilderness; what happens? He builds himself a log cabin or a sod hut; he works and endures hardship and deprivation; he clears land and plows it; perhaps he prospers. But what happens to the mind of a man thus uprooted, and to his children's minds? How long will it be—a thousand years?— before his children's children have the same bond with the new country that their ancestors had with the old? The sense impressions of centuries must be obliterated before sounds

and sights and smells gather full power and meaning. It will
be long before these people have the feeling as a symbol for
the goldenrod, say, that they once had for the rose or for
heather, for maize as well as for wheat. The still where they
make corn whiskey will not at once get the emotional hold
upon them that the winepress had. The mockingbird and
the hermit thrush will mean less to them than the nightingale had meant. When will the unfamiliar objects begin to
get a grip on them and take on symbolic content; when will
traditions, legends, myths gather about these novel things?—
for there is no better index than symbol, tradition, and myth.
No matter how a transplanted man may thrive in his pos-
sessions, his life is to some extent impoverished, even though
he may be quite unconscious of the deprivation, though he
may have disliked the old and may like the new: he once
had a close and vital tie with the world about him, and now
he has little or none, except as a source of a livelihood. His
treatment of the soil, his ruthless exploitation of it, and his
willingness to leave it and move on will be measures of his
lack of feeling.

His loss, however, in emotional relation with his natural
surroundings is by no means his greatest loss. Perhaps the
most important is social. He may settle among aliens—aliens
to each other as well as to him; and a number of strangers,
however friendly and kindly, cannot soon coalesce into a
close-knit community. Even supposing a whole community
migrates in a body, the communal life cannot go on; it speed-

ily disintegrates, because it was based upon the other locality.
Emigrants turn into detached individuals, like so many grains
of sand—but for a man to be severed from a social organism
is for him to suffer abnormal deprivation.

Furthermore, he finds his moral values altered. Possibly
he has to replace docility, obedience, loyalty, with independence, initiative, and hardihood. Here, of course, there may
be and no doubt often has been a gain; but often too the
process has ended in a bare and savage moral nakedness. At
any rate, the man's character has to be made over. And so
likewise his religion undergoes change. Even if he does not
feel that he has left the old gods in the old country, a new
life, a new character and morality, are bound to affect his
religion. How indeed should he sing the Lord's song in a
strange land?

In one form or another this is the story of the United
States. To be sure, the forms are many, and some of them
quite different from the typical instance given. Men and
women have come not only from English villages to the
virgin forests of Virginia and Massachusetts, from Norwegian fishing hamlets to the Dakota plains; they have
come also from Prague and Warsaw and Moscow to rural
Nebraska and New England, from Italian vineyards and
Rumanian farms to New York, Chicago, and San Francisco—
some early and some late. But in all the incalculable com-
plexity and variation of their experience there is at least one
common element: transplantation. One and all, they were

uprooted. Human adaptability, astounding as it is, has its limits; there is a kind of inertia in the mind. The difficulty of taking root again is not to be underestimated, nor of forming an organic community which provides all that communal life ought to provide. The individual may make an excellent superficial adjustment and get on well; but men's feelings, their basic desires and imaginings, are the deposits of centuries of racial experience. Below the surface, in the dim buried recesses of their minds, the "lone caves" are yet rife

> With airy images and shapes which dwell
> Still unimpair'd, though old, in the soul's haunted cell.

It is these "airy images" and old shapes which dictate the myths, the dreams, and the symbols of a people—which are the nuclei of their strongest and most profound emotions. How long a time must elapse before these are wholly assimilated to the new country?

All things considered, the process of assimilation has gone forward with amazing speed; nevertheless, it is still far from complete. Hardly one of us escapes the specific American conflict: the conflict between the American environment and our foreign heritages—I say "foreign" rather than "European," because many of us derive from Africa or Asia. Among us all, only the Indians have been here long enough to have become thoroughly one with the land. The rest of us still possess—or are possessed by—our alien patrimonies, deriving in all their appalling diversity from every region of the earth.

Yet they may be lumped together and called our foreign
heritage, which constitutes one of the main elements in the
making, the creation, of America.

The second main element, the land, the American environment, is almost equally diverse. It is a thousand envi-
ronments—forests, deserts, prairies, plains, mountains, with
all their climates—all at work molding men, shaping their
bodies, brains, habits, characters, occupations, attitudes, scales
of values, social organizations. Geography has obviously
helped make the types both of individual and of community
to be found in New England, for example, or in the Old
South; it has played its part in forming the cowboys of the
cattle ranches on the Great Plains, the trappers in the Rocky
Mountains, the hillbillies of Kentucky and Tennessee, the
farmers of the Mississippi Valley. Many of the effects of
environment are obvious, though seldom sufficiently considered; many are so subtle as to be undecipherable; always,
whether plain or obscure, they are momentous.

The story of America is the story of the process of interaction between the American country and the foreign heritage of the American people. This statement holds both
for the large manifest movements of national history and
for the hidden intricacies of individual psychology. The
fact of our alien origins is written large upon our landscape;
we have been doing our best to remake it, and have largely
succeeded, and meanwhile it has been equally remaking us—
both it and we resisting stubbornly and yielding only with

reluctance. The process is still far from complete, the conflict by no means yet resolved. Not until it is finished and the two terms fused or integrated into a unity will America achieve existence.

But this interaction or conflict has not been permitted to work itself out in peace. On the contrary, it has constantly been subjected to influences from the outside world; and here is the third term in the American equation. Isolation has been devoutly though mistakenly wished for but never attained by the United States, and the future promises even less isolation than the past has afforded. No major event on any other continent, no political or economic disturbance, no social change fails to affect us—no scientific discovery, no intellectual or artistic movement. From the days of Cromwell on, the course of our development has been modified by what was happening elsewhere—by the French Revolution, by the work of Darwin, by the painting of Cézanne and the novels of Zola, by events in Russia. For the present moment, probably nothing originating outside the United States is of so great consequence to us as the industrial era, the Power Age, which began in England. In fact, we imported industrialism with such alacrity and enthusiasm and carried it to such lengths as virtually to make it our own, in our own eyes and in the eyes of the world. For us of the twentieth century this element in our lives is so important as to take major rank, so that for us the struggle has become three-sided: between our foreign inheritance, the American environment, and the Power Age. Before the first two were blended, the third was thrown into the pot.

The typical story of the American may, then, be stated thus: He was uprooted from an old civilization, plunged into a primitive country, and before he got used to it, rushed into a world of airplanes, radio, and mass production. First, he found himself forced to revert to a more primitive level, to adapt his habits, his mind, his character to the wilderness, to become in brief something of a barbarian. That this change took place to a greater or less degree in the men of the early West is well known. There is reason to suspect that a somewhat similar change takes place among recent immigrants and their descendants in our great cities. Notoriously the second and third generations are less civilized than the original settlers or immigrants. The skin of civilization is likely to be sloughed off after transplantation and the naked savage who is just below the surface of everyone to make his appearance. The reversion to the primitive has not been confined to frontiersmen, though it has been most conspicuous on the frontier.

Yet the old heritage has not been completely lost. Even those men who "went Indian" to the point of scalping their enemies began at once to build a world modeled on what they had left behind. The pioneers lived not only in the savage present, but also in their memory of the civilized past, and above all in their anticipation of a civilized future. In part their dream has been realized; indeed we live in a civilization which goes far beyond anything they could have imagined. Yet it is also true that, since each newly created world has differed largely from the old, much has been lost—or, if not wholly lost, preserved only in our minds, sometimes consciously, more often unconsciously.

The frontier is gone, the pioneers are now behind us, and they too, as well as our remoter foreign ancestors, have bequeathed us a legacy, a legacy in conflict not only with our other, alien heritage, but also with the modern world we live in. Anyone who will contemplate the United States will observe several obvious results of this situation. The minds of the people are reflected in the face of the land: everywhere, from coast to coast, are to be found side by side evidences of original importations from Europe, of the original wilderness, and of the Machine Age. The mixture varies in degree, of course, between Virginia and Oregon: but even in New Jersey or Connecticut the land is only half tamed; even in Wyoming and Utah the people live in semi-European buildings and social organizations and listen to the radio.

So likewise in ourselves the three discordant elements coexist—and struggle. We cannot do without—we would not like to do without—mechanical inventions; yet we love and long for the primitive. Most of us could not and would not forsake our own country; yet we are more or less homesick for the Old World. When we cannot stand our cities any longer, we rush off on hunting and camping trips—until the wild is too much with us and we are delighted to rush back.

We sail by the million for England, France, and Italy—and are likely to be oppressed by the oldness of the Old World. Or, if we cannot escape in body, we take refuge in phantasy; if our own imaginings are not sufficient, we read of cowboys and trappers and outlaws, of glamorous bygone courts and castles. Sometimes we give physical form to these phantasies: I have seen service stations which were tepees, or quaint Norman cottages, quainter than anything in Normandy, marked "Ye Olde Gas Shoppe." We love antiquity, and savagery, and mechanisms. It would not be quite true, yet it would point toward the truth, to describe the Americans as a people who have gone primitive, live in ultramodern surroundings, and dream of ancient cultures.

Not that in this respect we are altogether a peculiar people; on the contrary, nothing about us is more interesting than the fact that we present in an enlarged and accentuated form universal human problems and difficulties. Everywhere men feel the discrepancy between the faulty present and their vision of a golden past. Europeans have irreconcilable pagan and Christian heritages to deal with, neither of which is in harmony with the modern world. And even in the most civilized of them the savage is buried only a layer or two deeper than in us. What order and stability and permanence they have achieved is only a strong enough illusion to make them forget that it is an illusion. Man from his birth on the steppes of central Asia or elsewhere has been an alien and a wanderer on the earth, looking for a home he can never find or make.

Insecurity, estrangement, and discord are his lot, and while he must go on struggling against them, it is well for him to be reminded that he need not look for success.

At the present time perhaps this reminder is superfluous, for the impact of industrialism and machinery has everywhere been sufficiently dislocating to disturb even the profoundest dream of peace. Nowhere has the new civilization been assimilated; Europe is suffering from the most acute indigestion—more acute, it may be, than ours. Yet, because we offered less resistance and were more quickly and more thoroughly conquered, the problem of adapting and reconciling humanity and the Power Age to each other seems to me clearer in this country than elsewhere, with the possible exception of Russia. The very fact that this conflict, along with the other universal conflicts, is so sharp and plain in the United States may give the best promise of resolution—so far as resolution is to be achieved at all anywhere.

The task is huge—out of these warring elements to create an ordered harmony, an integrated unity, which will be the United States. But other nations—Greece, England, France— once upon a time were faced with similar tasks, and did not wholly fail, though one may doubt whether they ever existed outside men's minds, save as botched approximations to an inner vision. The materials for the making of America have been assembled; it ought soon to be possible to catch some glimpse of the nation which the future holds in store—of the image toward which, though we never attain it, we shall be striving.   [1934]

The American Land

S AID THE Pawnee priest who was expounding his tribal ritual: "H'Uraru, the Earth, is very near to man; we speak of her as Atira, Mother, because she brings forth. From the Earth we get our food; we lie down on her; we live and walk on her; we could not exist without her, as we could not breathe without Hoturn, the Winds, or grow without Shakuru, the Sun."

When Smohalla, an Indian prophet of the far West, was urged to settle his people in agriculture, he replied:

"You ask me to plow the ground! Shall I take a knife and tear my mother's bosom? Then when I die she will not take me to her bosom to rest.

"You ask me to dig for stone! Shall I dig under her skin for her bones? Then when I die I cannot enter her body to be born again.

"You ask me to cut grass and make hay and sell it, and be rich like white men! But how dare I cut off my mother's hair?

"It is a bad law, and my people cannot obey it."*

Few white Americans have any such relation to the earth or any such thoughts and feelings about nature as the Indians. Like all primitives, the red men possess a strong sense of their identity not only with Mother Earth but with all nature.

---

* Hartley Burr Alexander, *Mythology of All Races: X. North American* (Boston, 1916).

[43]

The sky is their father and the father of all; the sun, the morning star, the winds, are spirits more or less like men, but more powerful; birds and beasts and plants are their kindred. All things are to be treated with a certain reverence, as one wishes, oneself, to receive consideration and respect. One breathes the air and drinks from the stream; one lives on corn and meat; should not these things be honored? And still more those beings which are the sources of spiritual power and of wisdom. Man is only one small member of a great society, in himself weak, helpless, unless aided by the other members. How long would he last if he were not fed and warmed and enlightened? As a dependent, it becomes him to render homage; as a kinsman, it becomes him to acknowledge the ties of relationship.

The ways of the paleface have struck the Indian as incomprehensible and outrageous. The white men killed the buffalo by the tens and hundreds of thousands and left their bodies to rot; white men have slaughtered all the game for the love of slaughter. They have cut or burned the forests. They have dug up the earth for minerals. The Indians lived always with a minimum of disturbance, fitting into the scheme of things, making themselves as inconspicuous as possible and hiding all their traces. But the whites upset everything as much as possible, totally changing the face of the land, sometimes out of sheer lust for destruction, always as if they gloried in the sense of power they got from leaving nothing as it had been. Like alien invaders, they came and raped a continent, and called it progress, civilization. They treated the country savagely, as an Indian might treat an enemy captured in battle; they tortured and enslaved it.

Not to revere, but to exploit: that has been the white man's primary wish toward his new country. He could not be expected to bring with him the primitive's religious veneration; but he did not even bring the natural piety of his ancestors for the soil. The land was strange and foreign to him, and he had come usually to get what he could out of it, often intending thereafter to return to his home. But he did not have everything his way: the conqueror frequently found himself made captive. If he persisted in his desire to exploit—as he might, for the opportunities were great—he fell under the fatal and ironical paradox which is the nemesis of all those who seek self-aggrandizement and the enhancement of the ego through the exercise of power: one is always mastered by that which one would master; one is the slave of that which one enslaves; one can buy this kind of power only by selling oneself for it. As a nation which subjugates another nation finds all its wealth and energy consumed in ruling the subject people, so a man who sets out on a career of exploitation finds that he must devote himself altogether to what he is exploiting; he must give his life to timber or copper or oil. In this way the American continent subdued those who undertook to plunder it. But the relation of the exploiter with nature, if it can truly be called a relation at all, is a sterile and destructive one.

Fortunately the desire for power can express itself through creation as well as through rapine, and many who came to conquer remained to love. They fell, often against their wills, under the spell of the new land. In Morten, the central figure of *The Emigrants,* Bojer has portrayed such a man. Morten left his Norwegian fishing village and came to the United States, to the Great Plains, in order to make enough money to return and get possession of his old home. But he found he could not go back for good, that the attachment he formed to his new country was just a little stronger than that to his old, and that he was torn between the two, as he discovered on his first return visit to Norway:

As he sped across the hills on skis and looked at the fairy-land of white woods, he felt that his soul was spellbound here forever. Even if he journeyed to the end of the world, he would always yearn and long for this. The hills, the fiord, the blue mountains lay there chanting night and day: "You are we. We are you. Wherever else you go, you will always be an alien." But another wave had caught him and was carrying him farther and farther away: the more he loved all this that was his own, the more he longed to leave it.

As an old man said to him: "I have been back to Norway seven times. . . . And each time I thought I was going back for good. . . . When you're here, you feel you can't be happy out of the old country, and when you've been there a little while, you begin to look out across the ocean, and you find that you're happier over here after all!"

The old man smiled mournfully; there was a far-away look in his eyes, as though they were always gazing across an ocean.

A heart so divided must have distressed many immigrants—nor is it confined to them alone, for they pass it on to their descendants. Sometimes, indeed, the pull of the old is felt most strongly by their posterity, reëmerging with overwhelming force. But commonly, as the generations pass, the bond grows weaker. It becomes a thing of the imagination only, and, unless constantly reinforced by reading or some such agency, tends to disappear. Yet a large percentage of Americans, even among those whose forebears migrated centuries ago, retain some trace of it, some nostalgia for the former homeland. They are inclined at odd moments to gaze with yearning across the ocean. Their hearts are not yet wholly one with the soil they live on.

What has finally held Morten and his like in this country has been the more open opportunity, the greater freedom they found for themselves in communities in the making; it has not been attachment to the strange new land. For the land was always foreign to them, and often repellent. Wherever they came from, they were unlikely to feel at home. Their feeling of distress has been excellently recorded in Rölvaag's *Giants in the Earth*—is indeed a major theme throughout the book:

It was a singular thing, not a soul in this little colony of Norwegians on the Plains ever felt wholly at ease, though no one referred to the fact or cared to frame the thought in words. All of a sudden without any cause, a vague, nameless dread would seize hold of them, it would shake them for a while like an attack of nerves; or again, it might fill them with restless apprehension, making them quiet and cautious in everything they did. They seemed to sense an unseen force around them. . . . Few realized what this strange feeling was; none of them would have admitted that he was afraid.

Millions of pioneers must have had such experiences, in the midst of an alien, hostile nature. As among Rölvaag's people, some have run away, back to where they came from; some have stayed and gone mad; and some have managed to adapt themselves, and to remake the wilderness in some partial conformity to themselves.

Not all pioneers, however, though all must have found their surroundings strange, have found them repugnant. Sometimes they have felt nature as the great antagonist, a worthy foe that, even during the encounter, they could not help loving. Willa Cather in her earlier stories, especially in *O Pioneers!*, shows nature in such a role; there are struggle and conflict, but the strife is heroic on both sides, and the final union is vigorous and strong. Out of such an initial opposition grows a powerful, productive relation. Sometimes pioneers, more especially I fancy if they are not immigrants but Americans with the tradition of the frontier, have felt their new environment as friendly from the beginning, not hostile, though strange—a new and unknown friend, of unwonted, potent possibilities. The central figure of Walter J. Muilenberg's *Prairie*—a novel the high merit of which has not received adequate recognition—has such a feeling for the wilderness where he settles. It is in part the novelty, the strangeness, which infatuates him; he possesses the impulse toward the distant and the untamed which turned so many Americans into perpetual frontiersmen, though this impulse

in him is dominated by the desire to make himself a permanent habitation:

Once, when there was this uneasiness in the wind, the man left his
accustomed place at the table and walked from the dim flare of
lamplight into the soft blackness outside. An elation seized him.
He lifted his face; he sniffed eagerly of the cool wet wind. The far-
away honking of the geese played over him with the thrill of a
dreamed melody. For him, there was ecstasy; still poignantly woven
into the phantasy of his delight, was a sense that he was not one
with this wild, lawless spirit.

If many Americans obeyed the wild, lawless spirit and followed the wild geese, many others, like this man, did not;
they stayed, though divided between two wishes, and made
a home for themselves out of the new land.

Perhaps the varying first contacts of pioneers with the soil
would be of little moment were it not that their experiences
are passed on and linger in one way or another among their
descendants and followers. The process of mutual assimilation between people and land which they begin continues so
long in their successors that it is nowhere yet complete. But
it does begin and go on; the land starts to remake the people
as quickly as they start to remake it. A tie between the two
is formed at once, and grows rapidly stronger; considering
the history and the heritage of Americans—not only their
foreign origin, but also their ceaseless wanderings,—I think it
surprising that there is as much attachment to the soil in this
country as there is. There would seem to be only two methods
of avoiding this attachment: one is to be always bent on ex-

ploitation and nothing else—for the exploiter forms nothing
that could be called an attachment,—and the other is to escape
into phantasy, to build up a refuge of imagination so seductive as to prevent any relation with one's actual world. That
this latter is a fairly common phenomenon in the American
countryside would appear from our fiction. It is part of our
literature of revolt, with its perverse preference for the mal-
adjusted. There has been a fad of writing about boys and
girls who, disgusted with the drab drudgery of farm life,
dream of the metropolis or of foreign parts or of some other
glamorous place they are ignorant of. The farmer's lot, as
everybody has been told, is not especially happy, and of
course all who wish to and who can should get away from it.
But likewise, if one is going to write about the country, or if
one has to live there, there would seem to be little profit in
a futile rebelliousness. Those who are able to make something of a go of it have the better of it both as human beings
and as material for literature. There is no special virtue in
lack of adaptation or adaptability, or in the indulgence of a
weakening phantasy.

It is only fair to say, however, that this strain, in spite of
a momentary vogue, is not dominant in American literature,
and presumably not in the United States. On the contrary,
both American people and American books are marked by
an extraordinary love of nature. This love may often be shal-
low, amounting to no more than the tourist's pleasure in
natural beauty; it need indicate no genuine attachment, no

real bond. Yet frequently it leads to the formation of endur-
ing ties. If American literature is peculiarly rich in nature
books, is it not because the numerous line of nature writers
of all sorts, from Thoreau and Burroughs to Ernest Seton
Thompson and William Beebe, have expressed a national
trait and responded to a national demand?

It may look odd that a people who have recently, as history
goes, moved into a new environment, should be so filled with
a love of nature; it may seem that attachment to a new soil,
contrary to what one would expect, is quickly made. But love
must be distinguished from sense of belonging, of kinship;
it is quite possible that the passion of Americans for nature
is saying less that they are at home than that they wish to
be at home. It may well be an effort to heal a breach. People
who are thoroughly at home, I suspect, have a deeper feeling,
less conscious and less vocal.

As it exists among us today—and its prevalence must not
be underestimated—it is a relic of the romantic movement,
which was a European reaction against too much civilization,
too much intellectuality—when I say "too much," I mean
more than men were prepared for, more than they could
stand at the moment. Their desire to be civilized beyond
their ability had divorced them from nature, had severed a
bond which ought never to be broken, and they rushed back
with all the ardor of long-absent lovers—and with all the illu-
sions and idealizations. Nature seemed to them charged with
divinity, a source of spiritual benefit and moral improvement.

America received the romantic view with enthusiasm, and the notion that nature is somehow ennobling and uplifting is still general among the American folk. Even those whose minds tell them something quite different about nature should not deceive themselves that they have freed themselves from the romantic feeling. And it may as well be admitted that there is value in this feeling—that the romantic movement would not have happened had it not answered a profound psychic need, a need of closer contact with nature. That need I take to have been and still to be even stronger in this country than elsewhere, because of our foreign origins.

This romantic love leads directly to that curious identification of the self with nature, that emotional and imaginative fusion, which runs throughout romantic poetry and which must have been experienced by thousands who were not poets. Shelley becomes the west wind, Keats the nightingale, Byron the storm in the Alps; each is "made one with nature." The psychological process involved is obscure, but seems to be somewhat as follows: nature is brought closer to humanity by being imaginatively mythologized—that is, mountain and wind and night and so on are imaginatively made into semi-human beings or spirits, are personified, have souls attributed to them; then the spectator, aware of a kinship between himself and these other beings, loses all restrictive sense of his own separate self and is conscious only of what he is witnessing. The experience is accompanied by a heightening of consciousness, a sense of freedom and enlargement; it is an ecstasy. Those in whom it is frequent tend to become mystics and pantheists, to develop a religion of nature worship. This type of religious experience, common everywhere in the nineteenth century, is almost the only kind to find expression in American literature. If one judged by our literature alone, that is, one would say that the only genuine religion the United States has had has been nature worship. Probably, however, the statement would be too extreme to be quite true.

It is significant that the romantic identification of self with nature implies an initial separation. One who lived always with a constant sense of his identity with nature could not have the experience. Not permanent union, but a reunion after having been cut off, produces the release, the sudden expansion, the ecstasy. The striking parallel between the romantic's and the primitive's relation with nature has been often noted; the romantic poet is the same kind of mythmaker as the savage, and the romantic religion of nature is close to the savage's religion. But the difference is equally important—and the two are as different as staying at home is unlike going home. More exactly, the savage arrives at his condition by development, the romantic by regression. For the romantic movement may be called either a reaction against civilization or an attempted regression to the primitive—and regressions, I suppose, are never satisfactory. To "go native" is no answer to the American demand for a closer relation with nature. In this matter, romanticism has done us more harm than good.

Another difficulty in our way is the modern intellectual theory of nature and of man, which is exactly the opposite of the romantic. Formerly, not enough good could be said of nature; nowadays, not enough bad. So far from seeming an emanation of the divine, nature now looks like

idle and ephemeral
Florescence of the diabolical—

looks like it, but is not, for nature in itself is neither good nor bad, but merely indifferent. When God, according to this view, disappeared from the universe, nature was seen to have no purpose or plan or meaning comprehensible to a human being. A soulless and senseless multiplicity of warring forces, it is heedless of humanity; but to men, whose demands it cannot fulfill and whose aspirations it thwarts, it appears not only ruthless but positively cruel. And indeed man's lot, in the midst of nature's vast negligence, *is* cruel; for man insists on high ends and a glorious destiny, but he is embarked only on "a blind atomic pilgrimage."

The modern view terminates in a singular paradox. On the one hand, it denies to man the special status and privileges, the immortal soul and the relations with God, which traditional religion had allowed to him; it holds that he is merely a subordinate and insignificant part of nature like any rock or bush or insect. His life has no import. He is wholly subject to and accounted for by natural forces and no others. Yet, on the other hand, he is at odds with the nature which brought him forth and to which he belongs; he cherishes cravings and hopes of which nature knows nothing; he is a queer waif or stray in an alien universe, a luckless vagary on nature's part, an anomalous changeling. As Joseph Wood Krutch says in *The Modern Temper,* man is "a fantastic thing that has developed sensibilities and established values beyond the nature which gave him birth."

If it is true that, though man is a mere product and parcel of nature, he and nature are hopelessly at strife, all notion of coming to terms and establishing beneficial relations with nature must of course be abandoned. But can it be true? Is man so completely anomalous, so utterly different from everything else? The evidence cited is that the scheme of things— if that phrase may be applied to what is schemeless—is not calculated to satisfy human longings. But what longings does it satisfy? Ask any animal, domestic or wild, whether all its wants are filled. If it could speak it would surely say that we humans have it pretty soft. And plants are no better off; they do not have everything their own way. Even inanimate things seem to possess tendencies which are thwarted. Man is no oddity; he is in the same boat with all other natural objects, and the fact that human longings are disappointed, so far from serving to set man apart, rather gives him a common bond with all things.

The proponents of man's queer and tragic singularity are misled because they have not freed themselves from the age-old assumption which they yet denounce—namely, that man has a special status. To be sure, they regard this status as calamitous and sardonic; but they do at least think man's plight peculiar. In their emphasis upon what they hold to be distinctively human they are still influenced by the centuries of Christianity and of humanism which lie behind them. They are deflated humanists; their creed is the last gasp of a dying humanism. But if man is not an alien at odds with nature, is rather thoroughly one with nature, in the realization of that oneness may be the possibility of hope and comfort.

When I say "one with nature," I do not mean that all is peace; I mean that man's disharmony with his surroundings is not confined to him but is the same disharmony that runs throughout nature. If man is dissatisfied, likewise is everything else. But to say that the quarrel is universal and that probably it cannot be completely solved is not to say that nothing can be done about it. Even in the United States, where for historical reasons the discord between man and environment has been unusually acute, the effort toward resolution need not be despaired of.

The goal—to be approximated, if never quite obtained—is the complete integration of the American people, alien in origin, and the American land. If the two are to be united, both land and people must be modified. As to the remaking of the land, I have little to say, except to point out that it has not been treated with sufficient respect. I have in mind, of course, the destruction of natural resources and the creation of much that is hideous and ill adapted to any humane purpose. Too many of our towns, for instance, are both ugly and unfitted to human life—partly because they were built without regard to the soil whereon they stand. In this remaking of the land, there are two considerations: one is that what we make should be what we really want—which it has often not been; the other is that it should be in keeping with the setting. Whether we really want Rhenish castles or not, we have no business putting them on Long Island. We have been too prone to transplant bits of Spain or Warwickshire or Bavaria to places where they do not belong—not in architecture only, but in all sorts of social organizations and customs. Bohemian peasants in Nebraska are equally guilty with Westchester millionaires. Our desires must be accommodated to geography and climate; we must accept the spirit of the materials in which we work, for the shape, and the lines, of the nation to be are already implicit in the soil. We, the people, need remaking worse than the land does.

[1934]

The Myth of the Old West

IN ALL the talks about the West—or the frontier, for the terms are synonymous—and about how it has "formed our character as a nation" for better or for worse, one aspect of the subject has been neglected: its value as a national myth or symbol. To be sure, the sweep across the continent from Jamestown to Oregon has often been called—and quite rightly—the American epic, and our own heroic age. The story of the West is our Trojan War, our Volsunga Saga, our Arthurian Cycle or Song of Roland. But these parallels are less likely to illuminate than to mislead and confuse; and in any case, what of it?

Its value, I should say, is, or rather might be, symbolic and mythical. I do not mean in the least to imply falsity. A story, true or not, which exerts a strange power over us, which becomes a nucleus about which cluster many feelings and imaginings—such a story I should call a myth. It is also a symbol, replete with significance. Indeed, as soon as its import can be analyzed and made explicit and rational, it is likely to lose its power.

Why nations and individuals profit from having their myths and symbols, it would be difficult to tell. Of course, the symbol gives form and body and vividness to much that would otherwise be formless and dim; it raises into consciousness what has been unconscious. Above all, it brings into actual manifest existence feelings, images, impulses, which before had existed only in potentiality, as music may be evoked from an instrument capable of music but hitherto silent. But why it is good for us to have these latent possibilities elicited is a perplexing question. I can only appeal to experience, and ask whether the kind of lift, of thrill, of quickening and invigoration, which comes when we are strongly affected by the power of a symbol, is not recognized as valuable.

Whether the West has any such power over Americans may well be doubted. One objection, sure to be raised, is that the old West was not actually heroic; to think of it so is to falsify and romanticize. There is undeniable truth in this objection; yet, for all that, it is based on a misconception. No age is in truth heroic, if "heroic" is taken to mean half-divine, superhumanly noble and magnanimous; King Arthur and Achilles were in reality barbarous chieftains, wild men, no doubt, sordid and grubby enough. But I am not sure that this is the meaning we of the present day ought to attach to "heroic."

Rather, I think, we should take it to mean strong in the primitive virtues—the animal virtues, if you like—physical vigor, physical courage, fortitude, sagacity, quickness, and the other qualities which enable a man to thrive in an uncivilized environment, to take care of himself amid primeval dangers and hardships. They are the individual, not the social, virtues. To us who live in a highly differentiated society, these traits are bound to seem heroic, because they survive in us as unused but strong potentialities, undeveloped because inappropriate.

Although the fact that so much of the savage is latent in us may make civilization precarious, we ought nevertheless to be thankful, for certainly we cannot afford to lose the primitive virtues. The frontier myth retains them in consciousness and provides them with exercise and activity, and not only keeps them out of mischief but makes their value available. We get back from the myth or symbol the "virtue" or potency which we put into it. This I take to be the function which the myth of a heroic age has always performed: it has embodied and preserved for a complex culture the values of a simpler world.

To date, the western story has not done all it might for us, because it has never received adequate representation. And no symbol can exert much force unless it is somehow objectified and worthily embodied. The story of the West should be the Great American Epic—does not everyone agree? Yet does anyone doubt that the epic is still unsung? A strange situation, surely, when the United States is full of able writers, and when these writers are unanimous in their neglect of what is unanimously called the grandest of themes. Something is wrong, and since there is nothing the matter with the story of the West, it is easy to see that the trouble must be with the writers.

Nor is it very difficult to see what that trouble is: by and
large, the better American writers are too highbrow. They
find Henry James more interesting than Jesse. Following in
the train of European leaders, they have spent their time
hunting the exact word, like Flaubert, or they have been
swamped by "a vast and desolating melancholy from Russia
or a perverse and astringent misery from Scandinavia." Like
Howells, they have fallen in love with the "foolish and in-
sipid face" of "real life." They have abandoned themselves to
trying to be subtle, minute, and accurate.

In a word, these Howells and James young men find the
West too strong meat for their stomachs. The western past
is violence and melodrama; it is peril and excitement, blood
and tears. To be sure, practically all the world's greatest literature is melodrama—danger, fighting, adultery, suicide, vengeance, infatuation, and murder. But such things have long
been out of style, on the supposition—disproved by any daily
paper—that they are not part of real life. The truth, I suspect, is that to write of the commonplace is easier, and that
authors have avoided more powerful stuff because they had
not the power to deal with it. However that may be, the
West was set aside, along with the rest of human life that
was not tame.

Furthermore, the West, after Bret Harte and Mark Twain,
came into literature through the back door, under auspices
that were undeniably lowbrow. The exploits of the James
brothers and of Buffalo Bill were retailed, by Colonel Pren-

tiss Ingraham and others, at ten cents a copy. The very success, commercially, of western stories has worked, by an odd twist, against their literary success. When Zane Grey and his compeers followed the dime novel and got rich, literary aspirants with serious purposes could not afford to soil their names by writing "best sellers." What would become of their reputations, if they wrote books anybody could enjoy? It must be said also that the public is partly to blame. It knew what it liked, and it knew that for the most part what it liked was not literature—especially the male half of the public, which above all liked tales of gunmen, scouts, and cowboys. The superstition, quite unwarranted—quite contrary to fact, indeed—grew up that western stuff was not the stuff of which literature is made.

Thus the "western" has suffered from a blight. A similar situation has existed in the movies. In spite of "The Covered Wagon" and a few other films, the "western" has been something that could not be taken seriously. Yet for the spectator it has been the most dependable kind of picture; during the dull seasons when Hollywood, in its magnificent isolation, has chosen to amuse itself by producing still-life studies of sex, one could always go see Tom Mix and Jack Holt galloping over the sagebrush. Thanks to "westerns," there have always been some movies in which something moved. And so it has been also with books. Zane Grey has always offered a refuge from the current studies in frustration and futility, in grease, drabness, and microscopic emotions. Yet

even the most ardent partisan of Zane Grey can hardly maintain that he has sung the great American epic.

The West, then, has suffered from providing a story too
good for modern literature; and it has also suffered from less
obvious causes. One of these is the curse of analogy. Jesse
James, for instance, is called the American Robin Hood;
and no sooner is he so called than the writer of Jesse's tale
goes looking for Maid Marian, and does well if he can leave
out Friar Tuck and give up brown October ale for red-eye.
Similarly, John G. Neihardt, who has written three long
poems of the West, is reminded by his subject of the *Iliad;*
and straightway rosy-fingered Aurora drives her chariot over
the Bad Lands, with steeds in place of cayuses, and Tithonus
sleeps in the Big Horn Mountains. Too few writers have been
willing to tell the story of the West in its own terms. Even
Zane Grey has looked through the eyes of a Sunday School
superintendent; his moral fervor has prevented him from
accepting his desperadoes and cowpunchers in their own
spirit: they must be improved and improving.

To be sure, there have been numerous books purporting
to deal with the historic West in its own temper. Thus Duncan Aikman has not felt that the story of Calamity Jane and
her fellow wildcats could be either improved or improving.
But the curse on these books is the curse of fact. They all
strive, or pretend to strive, for accuracy. But who wants facts?
They merely cramp the writer's style; he ought to busy himself with the glorified heroes of legend.

The blight which infects so many treatments of the West seems to extend even to a writer of such ability as W. R. Burnett, when he turns to western themes, as in *Saint Johnson*. That the author of *Little Caesar* and *Iron Man* could take the hardbitten, bloody feud of the Earps and the Clantons in the early days of Tombstone and make dry sawdust of it is incredible—but it has happened. No story—not that of Deadwood in its prime, nor of Abilene or Dodge City or Cheyenne, nor the life of Billy the Kid or Wild Bill Hickok— epitomizes so well the cold-blooded, wolfish ferocity bred by the frontier as the great feud of Tombstone; and the fact that it came so late—in the 1880's—serves to show that American lawlessness grew only the more deadly with the passage of time.

It is high time for the people of the United States to rebel against their recorders, and demand that some meaning be extracted from material so rich in significance as that concerning men or the children of men who left civilization and traveled the wilderness road. What really happened to these men? All America lies at the end of the wilderness road, and our past is not a dead past but still lives in us; thus the question is momentous. But it has not been answered. Our forebears had civilization inside themselves, the wild outside. We live in the civilization they created, but within us the wilderness still lingers. What they dreamed, we live; and what they lived, we dream. That is why our western story still holds us, however ineptly it is told.

It is an encouraging sign that one or two writers have attempted to answer that question, and to write of the West in its own terms. Harvey Fergusson's *Wolf Song* is almost what a "western" ought to be. His earlier novel of New Mexican life, *The Blood of the Conquerors,* portraying the defeat of the old Spanish order at the hands of the gringos, is an excellent novel but not a true "western." *Wolf Song,* however, has the proper ring; it is a good stiff story with plenty of excitement, and something of a legendary remoteness. Its mountain men are as salty as they ought to be, and the whole book is high in flavor—the flavor of the true "western." And it is admirably written, with a manifest delight which is itself delightful. A lyric yeast works strongly in both characters and author. Had it only, in addition, a certain magnitude it might be the great "western."

Mr. Fergusson's later novel of New Mexico, *In Those Days,* takes a pioneer through four stages of western development: "Wagons," in the days "when men would stop in the middle of the prairie to get married or have a fight or sing a hymn"; "Indians"; "Railroad," in the days of Hell-on-Wheels, "when a fancy woman was fancy and a good woman took in wash"; and "Gas," in the days of Ford. It is a lively book, crisp and vigorous, full of the right tang. The first part especially has much of the quality of *Wolf Song.* But Mr. Fergusson has surrendered to actuality. *Wolf Song* is a story able to stand by itself, independent of fact. *In Those Days* is a picture of social change, interesting as a portrayal of something that has happened, but dependent on historic data. Mr. Fergus-son has not cut loose and soared like one of his old-timers on a yarn-spinning spree. Perhaps he will do it yet, if he can conquer his truth-loving conscience, for he seems well equipped to make of the "western" what it ought to be.

And there is James Boyd's *Long Hunt*. Mr. Boyd indulges only in truth, bitter truth; yet in and through this actuality he has managed perfectly to project a symbolic image. This extraordinary novel, this harsh and tragic story, full of poetic and unsentimental beauty, is replete with a significance which eludes formulation. Its hero, in his zeal for freedom entrapped by his very effort to escape from fettering ties, is a type of all frontiersmen, yet a sharp-cut individual; the best Western character since Cooper's Leatherstocking, he is con-ceived with an insight and a subtlety which were not in Natty Bumppo's creator. So far as *Long Hunt* goes, it is a worthy embodiment of the heroic frontier myth; but its scope is narrow, limited to a single theme in a single character.

Many living writers are abundantly supplied with many virtues—honesty, sympathy and insight, literary skill. But most of them would be all the better off if they had more of the dynamic vigor and spirit, the dry, quizzical humor, the pungent earthiness, and the sentiment, too, which are all in the western tradition. These are the qualities needed for an achievement which American literature sadly needs. That achievement is nothing less than the adequate rendering, in its own terms and spirit, of the heroic age which popular phantasy has already created. The man who can do that, who can bring first-class individual imagination and emotion into key with national, will heal the lasting breach in our literature between lowbrow and highbrow, between writer and public, and give American literature such a basis for greatness as it has never had.

For this split between the nation and its literature is needless and harmful. It results from that sinister precision with which American artists avoid anything likely to touch the people. As I have said, they would be none the worse off if their work had more of the gusto and vitality of the "western"; and if to the representation of the frontier myth they could bring their skill, their insight and sense of fact, their honesty and discernment, the combination might produce great work. We know what Melville contrived to do in *Moby-Dick* with whaling, and what Stephen Vincent Benét has done in *John Brown's Body* with the Civil War. The story of the West offers better opportunities than either of those, as it is more nearly a true national myth. What is needed is the interpretation of it by the mature feeling, thought, and imagination of gifted individuals. Certainly the artist would gain from this union of his individual spirit with the national spirit; and the nation would gain, because at last it would have a fitly embodied image and symbol from which it could derive those values that belong to the myth of the heroic age.

[1929–1931]

Literature in the Doldrums

I: THE PAST

THE NEW REPUBLIC'S series of revaluations, last fall and winter, of American writers between 1911 and 1929 suggested strongly a question that was not answered: Where has all that literary activity left us now in the '30's? Mr. Cowley's concluding word was that the real achievement of those decades was to "create a new literary tradition," to "break a road for the writers who will some day follow them." If this were true, we should know where we are: it would be the business of present writers to continue the tradition and travel down the road. But suppose the reverse were the fact, that the tradition was ended and the road closed; then what? One cannot justly appraise the present situation without first examining its relation to the immediate past.

Unlike Mr. Cowley, I should say that the most striking thing about the writing of the 'teens and '20's, aside from the permanent excellence of much of it, is not that it points toward the future, but that it has swiftly and definitely receded into history. The "renaissance" of that period, like many other renaissances, was not a birth and a beginning, but an ending. Whenever numerous people, it seems, start singing "The world's great age begins anew," you may be sure that an era is dying. It is a law of literary history that these spectacular outbursts which look as if they were ushering in a new epoch are in truth ushering out an old one. It was so with the Elizabethans and the Romantics in England: first came the long slow fumbling preparation, then the sudden flowering. It was so even more conspicuously with the "Golden Day" in this country: Whitman thought he was a rooster crowing at dawn, but actually he was singing the swan song of the once triumphant ante-bellum democracy.

The analogy with the pre-Civil War literature of 1835–1855 throws still more light on the years 1911–1929, for it shows what fatal results too drastic a social upheaval can have upon writers. After the United States had transformed itself from a rural to an industrial society, Emerson, Melville, Whitman, and many others lingered on as forlorn ghosts in the Gilded Age, having survived into a world to which they did not belong and to which they had nothing to say. Writers belong to the years of their youth, and if the world changes too radically about them, they are reduced to impotence or silence.

A misfortune of this sort is what happened to the group with which we are concerned. Most of them were born in the '70's and '80's and were fully adult when the twentieth century began; almost all their best work is based upon their early experiences. After a brief flourishing, they all withered away. Mr. Cowley suggests that their promise was blighted by the World War. I should prefer to remark that their activity and decline coincided with the disappearance of the horse—though no doubt the coming of the war and the disappearance of the horse are related phenomena. The point is that all these writers belonged mentally to the years just before modern mechanism and industry reached their full development. Theirs was a horse-and-buggy literature; or, to speak in Lewis Mumford's terms, theirs was the "paleotechnic" age. And how they hated both it and the time which succeeded it! For what they voice is not the dominant attitude of the late nineteenth century, but a protest against it, and a protest furthermore, not from our point of view as we look back, but from the point of view of a still earlier day, of that earlier culture which was being crushed but had not yet been obliterated by the "robber barons" of the '80's and '90's. Witness the fact that the social criticism of Sherwood Anderson, Willa Cather, and Sinclair Lewis can be matched point by point in Emerson and Thoreau and even Cooper— in fact, Emerson is more modern than the later generation.

No wonder then that they hated machines and factories and mass production and all other peculiarly modern phenomena and that they withered away with the complete and final triumph of all these things! The world which had produced them and of and for which they wrote had disappeared. Survivors of a more individualistic society, they could make no contact with the new corporate and collective world founded on modern technics. For that such a transformation has taken place, except for cultural lags such as the persistence of private profits, is, I take it, the crucial fact of our days. To anyone who doubts it I recommend Lewis Mumford's *Technics and Civilization.*

This basic shift, then, from an individualistic to a corporate society crippled the writers of 1911–1929, because it killed the two main traditions or forces which animated them and gave them power. Concerning one of these two there is unlikely to be dispute: the old agrarian tradition and culture of the earlier United States, dominant before the Civil War, subordinate but still strong after it, so long but only so long as our supply of free land lasted. It was an individualism proper to an unclosed, uncircumscribed nation, a farmer's and craftsman's point of view. It was what most of us call "Americanism," the gospel according to Jefferson, Whitman, and the later Lincoln. And it still persisted powerfully in Robert Frost, Sherwood Anderson, Vachel Lindsay, Carl Sandburg, and many others. Of them all, only Sandburg has been able to make any sort of adjustment to modern industrial America; all the rest vanished with the social situation which had given birth to their spirit.

For the second of my forces I pronounce the obituary with less assurance: the cultural individualism, liberal and humanistic, which Joseph Wood Krutch and others have called, briefly and well, "Europe." So many men, with Mr. Krutch as chief mourner and eulogist, are standing by its grave and calling out "It is not dead but sleeping" that evidently they still cherish hope of a resurrection. Yet even Mr. Krutch once cogently demonstrated that its devotees were reduced to "mocking their torn and divided souls." And indeed this tradition looks as irreparably shattered as Humpty-Dumpty. It has disintegrated into bohemianism, dada, futility and despair, and sterile connoisseurship. Many of its followers have fled for refuge either to private phantasy or to the Roman Church. That any life should still cling to these pitiful fragments of a once great body looks improbable. As to why this disintegration has taken place, I suppose that Mr. Krutch gives the answer when he calls cultural individualism a luxury, a leisure-class affair, and that the economic system has tightened up to the point where the luxury can no longer be afforded. However that may be, the careers of Willa Cather and T. S. Eliot, to take only two instances, suffice to show what happened to recent Americans who chose the European road. They dwindled away as badly as the agrarians, and for the same reason: they all found themselves precipitated, as Miss Cather has recently pointed out, into an alien world.

No doubt many other traditions should be added to the chief two I have mentioned. But they all had two things in common; all were individualistic, and all are now bankrupt and exhausted. The naturalistic point of view, legacy of nineteenth-century science, especially of evolution, has vanished, even in its latest phase, Mr. Krutch's erstwhile "modern temper." "Psychological" literature, whether of inner phantasy or of streams of consciousness, has disappeared, save for the occasional batlike cheep of some still unlaid ghost. The "native Americans," having retired first to regionalism and then to history, grow more and more remote and faint, listening to lonesome drums along the Mohawk. Critical realism and satire have said their say on the defects of American civilization. The enumeration might be continued indefinitely.

I list these movements not merely to note that they are gone, but to serve as a reminder of how rich, how very much richer, the literary scene was twenty years ago than it is today. The many points of view which then sometimes struggled and sometimes fused together had been long rooted in experience, long matured; they were not bareboned theories, but ample elaborations of the feelings and imaginings of generations. In short, in their time they were good traditions; their irrelevance to the present should not make us forget it.

Nor should we forget the excellence of the writing to which they gave rise. To belong to history is no reproach; almost all the best writers belong there. We are inclined to make unreasonable demands on the immediate past. The early work of many writers is their best, and is not less good on that account. When I have spoken of certain authors dwindling away, it was as I might speak, say, of Melville, who dwindled away even more markedly. That he did so is nothing against *Moby-Dick,* and the later careers of their authors are nothing against *Jennie Gerhardt, The Man Against the Sky, Winesburg, Ohio, North of Boston, A Lost Lady, The Emperor Jones,* and *The Waste Land.* A period when each of a dozen or more people turns out some half dozen books of permanent value is no mean period in any literature. And the *New Republic*'s own revaluations show that these books are as good today as we ever thought they were. But with the individualism that informs them they have moved back into the past. Their very merits testify to the weight of history behind them and to the fact that they marked the end of an era. This fact, if true, is important because it means that at present in literature it is not up to us to carry on anything, but to make a fresh start. It becomes all the more vital to see what the ruling forces are nowadays—where at the moment we find ourselves.

Well, we find ourselves in the doldrums—if a doldrum is a place where calms and squalls abound, and baffling winds prevent one from sailing across the Line. Confusing puffs of air still sometimes blow out of the temperate zone we have left. The Line we are all trying to cross is of course the Equator which divides the individualist world from the collective; the trouble seems to be that while society in the main has crossed over even though its transit is far from completed, the corresponding transit of individuals' minds has barely begun. Both society and individuals are therefore full of conflicts with themselves and with each other. As a result even those writers who know where they want to go don't know how to get there—I mean, as writers. But one thing is sure, that not until they are able to ally themselves with forces active in the present world will they get anywhere at all.

II: THE PRESENT

Although literature today is in the doldrums, there are two groups at least of writers who are reacting as best they can to the new conditions of corporate society. As everybody knows, the literary movement of first importance in the '30's has been radical, revolutionary, Marxian, and even their opponents must admit that these people are trying to move on into the collective world and that they have leagued themselves with strong forces. Besides them, the only other movement of any consequence is the continuation, in changed forms, of what Mr. Cowley well called the "carnal mysticism" of 1911–1929—an attitude found then in Sherwood Anderson, Eugene O'Neill, Waldo Frank, and many others, including its high priest, D. H. Lawrence. Mr. Cowley said, "Little by little it disappeared from the main current of American writing." I wish Mr. Cowley were right; but is he? Has it not rather developed and changed from hatred of reason and intellectuality, from exaltation of "thinking with one's blood," into a glorification of the inevitable results of such "blood-thinking": into a cult of mere power and force, a cult of cruelty with its correlative pain and suffering, into a general waving of "the torches of violence"? Consider Hemingway with his bullfights, Faulkner with his human horrors, Jeffers with his birds and beasts of prey. I know that no one of these men has carried the cult to its logical and appalling limits; but isn't it true that one of their less scrupulous disciples would have a first-class time at a good lynching? Nowadays no one can doubt the final outcome of this state of mind: the Nazis have made that too plain. Presumably none of the gentlemen I have mentioned means to be, or is, a fascist—indeed, quite probably in a crisis they will be found fighting on the other side—but in their writing they have been prodding up the animals all the same.

Such then are the only two forces active in the literary scene, the only two responses so far to the new social situation. Compared to a quarter century ago, the present literary field looks singularly bare and empty. Not only have we far fewer active traditions to rely on, but the two we have are still harsh and crude, still undeveloped, at least in American literature—like young plants newly set out, unrooted and ungrown in the experience of American writers. One may grant that the experience of American workers has always been Marxian, and also, unfortunately, that too much of the opposition to them has been what nowadays would be called fascist. But to our writers these matters are pretty much stark ideology. How long a time is needed for concepts to take root and grow, one can see by considering the concept of evolution in the nineteenth century: the new idea was adopted quickly enough, but only much later was it digested and assimilated to men's feelings and imagination and view of life.

Not that the two present movements have no links with the past. Both the American agrarianism and the European

cultural individualism which I called dead did as a matter
of fact pass on much of their vitality, though transmuted
into collective forms. The rebellious spirit, the hatred of exploitation, the determination that every man shall have a
chance, of the agrarians have gone into the radical movements. To them also has gone much, perhaps all, that was
of value in the European tradition: the hatred of all that
is dear to the "bourgeois," the insistence that human values
and human development not only are more important than
profits and private acquisition, but are the very aim and end
of life. On the other hand, the ferocious and nationalistic
intolerance with which the old American way of life was
defended, and the bitter and snobbish class feeling which
has been implicit throughout European culture might easily
pass over to the "totalitarians." But in spite of these inheri-
tances neither of the two main groups of present writers is
yet sufficiently at home in the corporate world to do much
good writing.

The immediate apparent advantage may lie with the fas-
cistically inclined. The cult of blood-thinking, cruelty, violence, and power has more links with the past, involves less
novelty and change than its adversary because it is essentially
conservative and anti- (yes, or counter-) revolutionary. But
since blood-thinking means really no-thinking, unconsciousness, "bestial oblivion" and death of the mind, this cult seems
headed toward inevitable silence. Surely it cannot produce
much literature, for literature is by nature an elaboration of

thought and consciousness. Unawareness, stultification, insensibility, annihilation—these are after all monotonous and mute. In Jeffers and Faulkner a literature infatuated with death has gone into its frantic death flurry.

The ultimate advantage must lie with the radicals. So far from forswearing intelligence and knowledge, they use all they can get; it is all grist to their mill. Their world is not contracting, but expanding, and so are their minds along with it. Instead of propping up a decayed edifice or idly chronicling its collapse, they have faith that they are helping to build a fresh and sounder structure. They are on the side of life, of awareness and sensibility; no limits are set to the possibilities of their development. Furthermore, in socialist thought they have behind them a great European intellectual tradition. Yet they too are temporarily laboring under notorious difficulties as writers; they too are in the doldrums.

Most of them are recent converts, with all a convert's weaknesses as well as his zeal. They grew up saturated with individualism. They fatally neglected to get themselves born among the workers with whom their sympathies now lie. Their earlier literary passions are likely to have been Proust, Joyce, T. S. Eliot. As a consequence they are strong in enthusiasm and theory, but correspondingly weak in experience, and they pour their new wine into inappropriate old bottles because those are the only bottles they have. As has so often been pointed out, they are beginners, primitives, fumbling for a new mode of expression, like the English

dramatists before Marlowe, like most of the Romantic poets
before Wordsworth.

Yet, contrary to common belief, I think their fundamental
difficulty has to do, not with style and technique, but with
subject matter. Granted their radical viewpoint, of whom
or of what are they to write? Not of themselves or of others
as isolated individuals, for unlike the subjectivists they are
little concerned with their own or other people's unique and
private mental processes and phantasies; the subjective strain
has temporarily gone out. I say "temporarily" because some
day no doubt, with a better understanding of the individual
mind as a function of the social group, it will return. Unlike
the regionalists, again, they are not interested in quaint sur-
vivals of the past, or in history as a thing of the past. To be
sure, history reinterpreted in terms of the present might be
made to yield much, but so far the radicals have preferred
to make a direct attack on the center of their own time.

In middle-class life they have to date found their richest
material. Their best plays and novels have dealt with that
class: Odets' *Awake and Sing!*, Dos Passos' trilogy, Josephine
Herbst's *The Executioner Waits*. But excellent as much of
this writing is, especially Miss Herbst's, isn't the decline and
corruption of the middle class a somewhat limited theme?
By nature it is negative, and pathetic rather than tragic: the
struggle of people to keep things never much worth having;
their sufferings because they cannot keep up appearances; or
the rotting of personality in them if they prostitute them-

selves and prosper. And of course only these phases of the middle class interest the radicals. A somewhat different subject, and one richer in promise, is to be found in the relations between the middle class and the workers—in the shift of individuals, that is, from the one to the other. Stories such as that of Dos Passos' Charley Anderson, a good mechanic ruined by "the big money," have great latent possibilities. The corresponding change from the middle class to the radical or proletarian has been by no means exhausted; it has been but barely touched in the plays *Waiting for Lefty* and *Peace on Earth,* and among the minor characters of Miss Herbst's novel. Since our writers commonly have middle-class backgrounds, they are likely to find their best material in these subjects.

From such considerations the question of the farmer ought not to be omitted. Hamlin Garland's *Main-Travelled Roads* might well be traveled again. Since he wrote, nearly fifty years ago, we have had little incisive treatment of farm life. Of late the countless sagas of the soil have been getting more and more idyllic, while the actuality (except for relief measures) has been getting grimmer and grimmer. Here is more significant drama and more moving tragedy than in the decline of the middle class; here is a chance for the radicals, the potentialities of which Miss Herbst has already made plain in a few brief but superb episodes. So many writers have grown up on farms that they ought to be well equipped for this task.

But of course all the radicals want to write about the workers—if they only knew how. And they are right in their wish, for here is the great unworked material; here is strong meat, for anyone who could assimilate it. But it is just here that writers' troubles with experience, theory, and technique come to a head. The chief obstacle is that so few of them belong to the proletariat. Perhaps they can make up for this deficiency by deliberate effort and by imagination; Dos Passos, for instance, succeeded with his I.W.W. typesetter, Mac, in *The 42nd Parallel*. But unless a novelist can somehow absorb the necessary experience until it is wholly part of himself, he had better not try to write proletarian novels, for neither his theories nor his technique will help him. The reason is that both the theory and the form must emerge from the material itself. But in most "proletarian" literature the style seems to be laid on from the outside and to fit badly, as in Joycean or Proustian studies of lumberjacks and longshoremen; and the whole work looks devised to exemplify general ideas, as in oldfashioned Sunday School tracts. Yet I have confidence enough in radical theories to believe that they will be found implicit in the facts if honestly presented; and I am sure that form and style can be pretty much left to take care of themselves.

In his aesthetic parable of the axe helve, Robert Frost pointed out that   the lines of a good helve
　　　　Were native to the grain before the knife
　　　　Expressed them, and its curves were no false curves
　　　　Put on it from without. And there its strength lay
　　　　For the hard work.

So it is with a story or a play. A writer sufficiently possessed by an absorbed experience need only be true to it. A notion is abroad that none of the technical achievements of bourgeois fiction must be allowed to lapse; but could anything be falser? Every new kind of art demands a new kind of expression growing out of the new substance and point of view. It requires a genuine fresh start, a sort of "return to nature," a going back to beginnings.

That is why I deplore any idea that present writers should try to continue the tradition or travel the road followed in 1911–1929. On the contrary, they need to begin at scratch—at the original facts—and at first to be not too ambitious. Our minds are still so far on the individualistic side of the line that divides us from collectivism that it is too early for panoramic treatments of masses and classes. What we need is plain, simple, direct writing about individual American workers—their typical lives will bring in enough of the "corporate" and "collective,"—bald and rough in style if necessary, but at least authentic and unvarnished and not "literary." During the World War in an army hospital I heard my fellow patients tell such stories by the hundreds, and they were better stories than any proletarian literature I have yet seen. The tellers weren't worrying about their narrative technique; they didn't mean to be "Marxian," and were on that account all the more effectively so. They merely told what they and other people had said and done. Here was the elemental stuff of their experience in their own words. It needed only pruning and compression to be literature. A writer who could begin at this point could give American literature the impetus it needs to get out of the doldrums.

[1937]

Dos Passos and the U. S. A.

THE CHOICE of the ambitious title *U.S.A.* for the volume which brings together Dos Passos' *The 42nd Parallel, Nineteen-Nineteen,* and *The Big Money* looks as if it might be intended to stake out a claim on the fabulous "great American novel." And Dos Passos' claim is not a weak one. A single book could hardly be more inclusive than his: in the stories of his main characters he covers most parts of the country during the first three decades of the twentieth century. His people have considerable social diversity, ranging from Mac the I.W.W. typesetter and Joe Williams the feckless sailor to Ben Compton the radical leader, Eleanor Stoddard the successful decorator, Margo Dowling the movie star, and J. Ward Moorehouse the big publicity man. The background of the panorama is filled out with "newsreels" of newspaper headlines, popular songs, and the like, with the autobiographic "camera eye" which gives snatches of Dos Passos' own experience, and with a series of biographical portraits of representative men—Debs, Edison, Wilson, Joe Hill, Ford, Veblen, Hearst, and twenty more. Probably no other American novel affords a picture so varied and so comprehensive.

Furthermore, the picture is rendered with extraordinary vividness and brilliance of detail, especially of sensory detail. Sights and sounds and, above all, smells abound until the reader is forced to wonder that so many people, of such different sorts, are all so constantly aware of what their eyes and ears and noses report to them: might not some of them, one asks, more often get absorbed in meditation or memory or planning or reverie? But it is no part of Dos Passos' scheme to spend much time inside his characters' heads; he tells, for the most part, what an outsider would have seen or heard—gestures, actions, talk, as well as the surroundings. The result is a tribute to the keenness of the author's observation—not only of colors, noises, and odors, but, even more important, of human behavior and of American speech. People as well as things are sharp and clear and distinct.

Nor does the presentation lack point and significance. As the book goes on, the U.S.A. develops, with the precision of a vast and masterly photograph, into a picture of a business world in its final ripeness, ready to fall into decay. Though Dos Passos does not call himself a Marxist—and would seem in fact not to be one—his point of view is unmistakably radical. The class struggle is present as a minor theme; the major theme is the vitiation and degradation of character in such a civilization. Those who prostitute themselves and succeed are most completely corrupted; the less hard and less self-centered are baffled and beaten; those who might have made good workers are wasted; the radicals undergo internal as well as external defeat. No one attains any real satisfaction. Disintegration and frustration are everywhere.

The whole presentation leads to the summary: "Life is a shambles." Perhaps there are implications that it need not be; but no doubt is left that actually it is.

These generalities, when stated as generalities, have of course become the trite commonplaces of a whole school of literature. But actual people shown going through the process of victimization can never become trite or commonplace; the spectacle must always be pitiful and terrible. And no one, I should suppose, could look on Dos Passos' picture wholly untouched and unmoved. But still one might ask whether he had quite achieved the tragic effect which presumably he aimed at.

To complain that the picture is one-sided may appear captious and unreasonable, and in one sense of "one-sided" it is. The whole truth about a hundred million people throughout thirty years cannot be told in fifteen hundred—or in fifteen million—pages. The novelist has to select what he considers representative and characteristic persons and events, and if Dos Passos has chosen to omit big businessmen, farmers, and factory workers, and to dwell chiefly on midway people in somewhat ambiguous positions—intellectuals, decorators, advertising men—perhaps that is his privilege. The question is whether this picture of his, which is surely extensive enough as novels go, is entirely satisfactory within the limitations which must be granted. How close does U.S.A. come to being a great American novel? That it comes within hailing distance is proved by the fact that it has already been

so hailed; indeed, it comes so close that the burden of proof
is on those who would deny the title. Yet to grant it offhand
would be premature.

On one point at least everyone probably agrees: that the
biographical portraits are magnificent, and are the best part
of the book. But wherein are they superior? Is it not that these
portraits have a greater depth and solidity than Dos Passos'
fictional characterizations—a more complete humanity? If so,
the implication must be that his creation of character is not
complete. And indeed when Mac is put beside Big Bill Haywood, or Ben Compton beside Joe Hill and Jack Reed, or
Margo Dowling beside Isadora Duncan, the contrast is un-
flattering to Dos Passos' powers as a novelist. There is more
human reality in the ten pages given to Henry Ford than in
the twenty-odd given to Charley Anderson. Nor is the explanation that the real people are exceptional, the fictitious
ones ordinary, satisfactory: some of the fictitious ones are supposed to be leaders; and besides, it is a novelist's business so
to choose and treat his imagined characters as to reveal his
themes in their utmost extension, not at their flattest. No; the
contrast has nothing to do with the positions people occupy:
it is a fundamental matter of the conception of human nature
and the portrayal of it in literature.

In thinking of this contrast, one notices first that the real
men have a far better time of it in the world, that they do
find a good many genuine satisfactions, that even when they
fail—when they are jailed like Debs or shot down like Joe

Hill—they are not wholly defeated. Inside them is some motive power which keeps them going to the end. Some of them swim with the stream and some against it, but they all swim; they all put up a fight. They all have persistent ruling passions. Furthermore, they are all complex and many-sided, full of contradictions and tensions and conflicts. They have minds, consciousness, individuality and personality.

Not that all these things are entirely lacking in the fictitious characters—Dos Passos is too good a novelist for that,—but they do appear only in a much lower degree, played down, degraded, reduced to a minimum. As a result, the consciousness of these people is of a relatively low order. True, they are aware with an abnormal keenness of their sensations; but is not this sensory awareness the most elementary form of consciousness? On the other hand, these folk can hardly be said to think at all, and their feelings are rather sharp transitory reactions than long-continuing dominant emotions. Above all, they are devoid of will or purpose, helplessly impelled hither and yon by the circumstances of the moment. They have no strength of resistance. They are weak at the very core of personality, the power to choose.

Now it may be that freedom of choice is an illusion, but if so it is an inescapable one, and even the most deterministic and behavioristic novelist cannot omit it or minimize it without denaturing human beings. When the mainspring of choice is weakened or left out, the conflicts and contradictions of character lose their virtue and significance, and personality almost disappears. Dos Passos often gives this effect—that in his people there is, so to speak, nobody much at home, or that he is holding out on us and that more must be happening than he is willing to let on. This deficiency shows itself most plainly in the personal relations of his characters—they are hardly persons enough to sustain real relations with one another, any more than billiard balls do—and in his treatment of crises, which he is apt to dispose of in some such way as: "They had a row so that night he took the train. . . ."

The final effect is one of banality—that human beings and human life are banal. Perhaps this is the effect Dos Passos aimed at, but that it is needless and even false is proved by the biographical portraits, in which neither the men nor their lives are ever banal. The same objection holds, therefore, for Dos Passos' whole social picture as for his treatment of individuals: that he has minimized something vital and something which ought to be made much of, namely, forces in conflict. Society is hardly just rotting away and drifting apart; the destructive forces are tremendously powerful and well organized, and so are the creative ones. Furthermore, they are inextricably intermingled in institutions and in individuals. If Dos Passos is forced, by sheer fact, to present them so when he writes of Ford and Steinmetz and Morgan, why should he make little of them in his fiction? Is it to illustrate a preconceived and misleading notion that life nowadays is a silly and futile "shambles"?

One might hope, but in vain, to find the answer in the

autobiographic "camera eye." To be sure, the author there appears as the extremest type of Dos Passos character, amazingly sensitive to impressions, and so amazingly devoid of anything else that most of the "camera eye" is uninteresting in the extreme. The effect of this self-portrait is further heightened by the brief prologue which introduces *U.S.A.*: an account of a young man, plainly the author himself, who "walks by himself searching through the crowd with greedy eyes, greedy ears taut to hear, by himself, alone," longing to share everybody's lives, finding his only link with other people in listening to their talk. If the obvious conclusion could be accepted that Dos Passos had been never a participant, but always a mere onlooker hungry for participation, so that he had to depend only on observation from outside, it would explain much. But such is not the fact: he took part in the World War and in the Sacco-Vanzetti case and other activities. He has been no mere spectator of the world. Moreover, he must have had powerful and lasting purposes and emotions to have written his books, and it is hardly credible that he has done so little thinking as he makes out. His self-portrait must be heinously incomplete, if only because he is a real man. But it is possible that he may have chosen to suppress some things in himself and in his writing, and that he may have acquired a distrust of thought and feeling and will which has forced him back upon sensations as the only reliable part of experience. Some such process seems to have taken place in many writers contemporary with him, resulting in a kind of spiritual drouth, and in a fear lest they betray themselves or be betrayed by life. Perhaps the disillusionment of the war had something to do with it, but more probably a partial and one-sided view and experience of our present society is responsible.

According to any view, that society, in all conscience, is grim enough, but not banal, not undramatic. Dos Passos has reduced what ought to be a tale of full-bodied conflicts to an epic of disintegration and frustration. That reduction—*any* reduction—is open to objection, because it is an imperfect account of human beings and human society that does not present forces working in opposition. In that sense, *U.S.A.* is one-sided, whereas life and good literature are two-sided or many-sided. In a word, what we want is a dialectic treatment of people and the world. Dos Passos does not call himself a Marxist; if he were more of one, he might have written a better novel. The biographical portraits are the best part of his book because they are the most nearly Marxist, showing the dynamic contradictions of our time in the only way they can be shown, namely, as they occur in the minds and lives of whole men. Nothing will do, in the end, but the whole man.

[1938]

Jack London—Wonder Boy

"I HAVE LET Jack London tell his own story in his own words," says Mr. Stone, presumably to explain the inclusion in his biography of long passages from London without quotation marks. "Where Jack told the truth about himself, no biographer could possibly tell it better or truer. . . . There is nothing of the biographer in *Sailor on Horseback*."

In the last sentence Mr. Stone does himself injustice: he has at least got for the first time into print the main facts about London's birth and death—his illegitimacy, and his suicide. But in the main the modesty of Mr. Stone's statement is vindicated, and he has contented himself with reproducing once more his hero's self-portrait. This method, which has been used with the greatest success by Van Wyck Brooks, though with the striking difference that Mr. Brooks has explained his procedure in the body of his books and Mr. Stone has not, is unexceptionable in itself. Its value, however, depends not only on the skill and perspicacity of the biographer, but also on the self-knowledge of the subject, and on that point Jack London presents extreme perils. His "self-dramatization," to which Mr. Stone refers, led him so persistently to romanticize and glorify himself that one ends by asking whether he ever "told the truth about himself"—or for that matter, since he equally romanticized the world, about anything. The answer must be that on occasion, when Jack wasn't looking, truth did creep into the corners and crannies of his writing, though almost never when he was contemplating his own image.

The first objection to *Sailor on Horseback* is that London has fooled Mr. Stone as completely as he fooled himself; the second is that the biographer has caught from his subject that falsity of style, of the early Hollywood, "Came the dawn" school, which was the perfect, the inevitable expression of Jack's peculiar romanticism—the taste which made him call his wife "mate woman" and himself "God's own mad lover." To these phrases Mr. Stone objects, but seems not to see that this overpitched, hectic quality infects more or less not only all of London's work, but his own writing too. Mr. Stone is capable of referring to "life raw and naked, wild and free," and of describing Jack's reading in these terms: "He sank his teeth into the throat of the book, shook it fiercely until it was subdued, then lapped up its blood, devoured its flesh, and crunched its bones." Mr. Stone is also capable of saying that in the year 1900 humanity "wandered shatter-brained in the miasmic fogs of the Dark Ages." Perhaps these passages are pure London, verbatim; but I think that Mr. Stone has gone his hero one better.

Though *Sailor on Horseback* is the best, being to all intents and purposes the only, life of Jack London to date, it is no "definitive biography"; it shares too fully the delusions, the naïveté, the feverish inflation, the unreliability, of its subject. London needs critical treatment, done from the outside, and he is a figure of enough interest to deserve it.

But to disentangle the facts from his phantasy of himself would be almost impossible. There is no question that he was a precocious boy, with an excellent physique and a brilliant mind, and that as a man he was eminently, even excessively, sociable, generous, kind, and likable; it might as well also be said that he had the writer's gift with words, the literary genius, as well as, unfortunately, a genius for self-deception. He was, I should judge, a potentially great man, whose possibilities of greatness were almost wholly wasted. His was a double tragedy, public and private: he never did the work he was meant for, and his own life ended in failure. At the root of both lies the phantasy which ruled him—the regressive myth of the primitive, barbaric hero.

The myth, of course, is universal. All boys want to be and play at being outlaws, pirates, highwaymen; no doubt it is part of their resistance to growing up and becoming civilized. And probably there is no harm in living out the myth somewhat in adolescence—there may be good in it. But most grown men put it behind them, except for their reading— how widespread a phantasy it remains in all modern nations there could be no better evidence than Jack London's own popularity. The only thing that distinguishes him from the majority is that he was ruled by it all his life, and that more than other men he wished and was able to live it out. The phantasy which dominated him led him straight away from organized society to "hit the adventure trail"—into oyster piracy on San Francisco Bay, into seal hunting on the Pacific, into hoboing, to the Klondike, to the South Seas. When not entirely beyond the pale, he lived in a pseudo-artistic bohemia. His final effort—to found a vast patriarchal domain—was hardly less primitive than his other ventures. His constant need was to be or at least to imagine himself a swaggering lord of creation, a glorified superman; and by necessity as well as by choice, he was driven, in order to play this role, out of the civilized world. For civilized people he had no use, anyway; they were effete mollycoddles. Darwin, Spencer, Nietzsche all showed him, he thought, the superiority of the blond beast, the Nordic hero.

His personal tragedy sprang, apparently, from his most peculiar trait: his extraordinary combination of a fine body and overfine nerves. Without such a body, he would have had, like most men, to let the phantasy remain a phantasy. Without the overstrung nerves, he would not have driven himself to destruction trying to realize in actuality an adolescent dream. Ordinarily one takes a febrile overexcitement and love of excessive violence to be signs of weakness; but in Jack London they were not—he really did have strength. So likewise in his writing: his fury of language and intemperance of emotion have led some critics to deny that he possesses genuine vigor and power. But to do so is surely an error; those who are not too much offended by his excesses can hardly fail to feel his force. Only, in his books as in his own life and character, the strength he had is turned, as if he could realize it only in fighting, coercion, and destruction, not to creation, but to violence. To so little good use did he put his abilities in his work that his intrinsic literary value is not great; mainly he is of interest as a social phenomenon.

London manifests with particular clarity the contradiction, the duality, or two-facedness, which runs through all naturalistic American writers and which is presumably an expression of the basic contradiction in the society from which they came: on the one hand they are extremely social; on the other, highly individualistic. So Dreiser is the former in *An American Tragedy* and the latter in *The Titan*. So during the decades when men born in the 'seventies were growing up, the United States was treated to a riot of unbridled individualism in the business world by the robber barons—thoroughly commonplace men permitted by historic circumstances to enact amazing parts—at the same time that society was being collectivized, by these very same men, as never before. That both elements were strong in Jack London he knew as well as anyone, and made no attempt to reconcile them: Marx and Nietzsche reveled side by side in his mind. To be sure, he said: "I am Martin Eden. Martin Eden died because he was an individualist, I live because I am a socialist and have social consciousness." Though in the end he followed Martin Eden to suicide because his social consciousness was too weak to save him, it is true that he did have it and that he was a socialist—about ten per cent of him, at least.

In view of his socialism, nothing is stranger than his treatment of the workers. He liked to call himself one of them, born and bred in the working class, but herein he was, as so often, merely deceiving himself. He came from the bottom—not to say the lunatic—fringe of the middle class, and he was a worker as little as possible, never holding a regular job for more than a few weeks, and always feeling as much contempt as pity for "work beasts." Nor as a writer did he much concern himself with the proletariat; the only important exception is the first part of *The Valley of the Moon,* though it is true also that perhaps his best writing—and his only realism—is to be found in the realistic portraits of minor figures who are proletarians. He was attracted to socialism not because he was a worker, but because he was rebellious, gregarious, and sympathetic, humanitarian and idealistic, because socialist arguments carried intellectual conviction, because he admired some groups of workers for their spirited brawniness, and above all because in the labor movement, as for instance in strikes, he found the violence he loved, and the promise of far more violence to come. In his phantasies of the future dealing with general strikes and such things, it is the violence, not the significance for labor, that he dwells on and gloats over. The career of such a man as Big Bill Haywood, one would think, might have appealed to him as a literary theme; but, knowing nothing of the labor movement from the inside, he would in any case have been incompetent to deal with it. Besides, though there was enough of the socialist and enough sympathy with labor in Jack London to establish his connection with the collective side of the society he lived in, his heart and his imagination were really elsewhere.

He was at least ninety per cent individualistic—far more so even than other naturalistic writers, who all, when not showing their characters as helpless victims of social forces, liked to portray them as supermen. For all these writers had heard of Darwin and had read Huxley and Spencer; they all knew about the struggle for existence and the survival of the fittest; they all believed, as London did, that they arrived at this view of things by thinking with remorseless logic from the "irrefragable facts" of science. But one must suspect that their observation of the world carried more weight and was more fundamental than their readings in popular science; for never had life been so obviously Darwinian, so naturalistic, as in the American business world of the Gilded Age.

Unlike Dreiser, it is true, London did not fall for the business titan, partly because he was a socialist, but mainly because the values of capitalism always antagonized him: much as he liked to spend money, he detested the qualities which ordinarily lead to moneymaking. His attitude comes out most clearly in *Burning Daylight*, of which the hero, an Alaskan superman of the typical London sort, returns from the Klondike with a fortune, by primitive methods puts the anemic, unmuscular financiers in their place, becomes himself a robber baron at the expense of his soul, and finally throws away his money and flees from the world to make a bare livelihood on an out-of-the-way farm. Yet, with all its criticism and rejection of business, this novel makes pretty plain the underground connection between its author's individualism and that of the Gilded Age—a connection made plain also in *Martin Eden,* and even plainer in *The Iron Heel,* in which the leading industrialist is a Wolf Larsen of business and is recognized, though as an enemy, as at least a worthy and in a sense a kindred enemy.

Still other aspects of his special time and place made their contribution to Jack London's peculiar and paradoxical literary blend. One of the most important was the frontier, which was not far away from California in the 1870's, and with which both his mother and his foster father had affiliations. An obvious sign of his heritage is his fondness for frontiers—Alaska, the South Seas—and frontier conditions and types, for men who have escaped the fetters of civilization, for outcasts and outlaws. Another is his agrarian streak, his preaching of a flight to the land. His attitude toward businessmen is a frontier attitude. And probably his obsession with the hero myth, which among Americans has usually embodied itself in frontier terms, is partly derived from the same source. But the frontier has been much too exclusively emphasized in connection with American literature; one must not forget, particularly with Jack London, that other sources may be of considerably more consequence.

Of these I should like to suggest that for him the most significant is his relation with the lower middle class. In it he originated and grew up, and first and foremost he was its spokesman. If a census of his readers could be taken, I have no doubt a majority of them would be found there, especially in the white-collar group. To those whose lives are dreariest and most tedious, struggling to keep up appearances on the meagerest livelihood and maintain a precarious status, he offers the perfect vicarious satisfaction. His heroic phantasy is the compensatory myth, above all, of this class; to it his romantic naturalism is strong meat and drink. I do not know that it has been pointed out how much there is in London of a bastard nature mysticism, of exulting in and worshiping and getting drunk on "the wine of life"—in short, of "blood thinking." The very titles of his books are full of it. Although naturalism ends in pessimism, futility, and despair, it begins with rejoicing in strength, or strength through joy—*Kraft durch Freude,* to use the Nazi phrase. The turning of power to violence—Jack London's forte—in fighting, coercion, and destruction, is also the specialty of the lower middle class in its sporadic outbreaks, its happy reversions to savagery in lynchings and vigilante activities. By this time everybody ought to know that this trait of this class is, quite literally, the most dangerous thing in the world today: and what writer feeds it better than Jack London? No wonder he has been popular in Germany: most of his books might well be taught in the Nazi schools. Even the glorification of race is in them, if "Anglo-Saxon" were changed to "Nordic." As for his attacks on big business, they would have to be deleted now—but in the early days of the movement the Nazis would have applauded them. If there is such a thing as the "fascist unconscious"—and I fear there is—it is the product and property of the lower middle class, and Jack London shared it. Fortunately, it was only a part of him, though the major part of his work; also in him, in utter contradiction, were its opposites.

This conflict of opposites is clearest in what is nowadays by all odds his most interesting and important book: *The Iron Heel,* published in 1907, the best anticipation of fascism yet written. Though sheer phantasy, not nearly so fully created and embodied as *It Can't Happen Here, The Iron Heel* is a far better book because London understood the subject much better than Lewis, in spite of the greater knowledge available to Lewis. *The Iron Heel* represents a great feat of imagination; its only important omission is the part played by the lower middle class in fascism, and its prophecies are amazing, as for instance the role of the "labor aristocracy." The chieftains of the A. F. of L. would do well at this moment to read this book with searchings of heart. . . . *The Iron Heel* is not, however, the outcome of pure imagination working in a void. London had a good deal to go on. He knew the history of labor in the United States. He has his industrialist say to the socialist leader:

When you reach out your vaunted strong hands for our palaces and purple ease, we will show you what strength is. In the roar of shell and shrapnel and the whine of machine-guns will our answer be couched. We will grind your revolutionists down under our heel, and we shall walk upon your faces. The world is ours, we are its lords, and ours it shall remain. As for labor, it has been in the dirt since history began, and in the dirt it shall remain so long as I and mine have the power.

The words are the words of Jack London, but the purport is the purport of—anybody can supply names.

London knew that always, when labor had become active, it had been met and repressed with lawless violence. Before and during his day as much as in ours, labor in this country was met by fascism; "it has happened here," over and over again, that employers have hired private armies and aroused the lower middle class to beat and shoot the workers. So London had only to project the familiar phenomena of American life on a vaster scale into the future. Above all, moreover, he had only to project into the future what he found in himself; in his own mind and heart were all the ingredients of the conflict, the forces of his own time to which he was so responsive and which were headed toward the struggle he depicts: socialism and sympathy with organized labor on the one hand, on the other ruthless individualism and disregard of social welfare, and a passion for power and violence.

To estimate the value of Jack London's work is not easy. As pure literature it is small—but perhaps literature had better not be too pure. Perhaps it may be granted that so far as the social consciousness he claimed for himself appears in his writing, it is all to the good. There is much also to be said for his portrayal of the jejune, sterile character of traditional American culture. Furthermore, his criticisms of capitalism and business are not, to say the least, to be quickly dismissed. But as to the main features of his work—the phantasy of the primitive hero and the love of violence—it is hard to say. Many readers, no doubt, will decide that the heroes are stupid and the violence dangerous. And so they are. But can so wide-spread a myth be entirely without value? Must it not preserve something worth preserving, for which there is no room in actual life? Few people will take these blond beasts altogether seriously; but equally few would dare to have the elemental barbaric virtues they embody disappear from the world. Physical stamina, physical courage and endurance and hardihood—the "wild and free" strength which has so little place in our business civilization,—surely these things are good in themselves, and there is no telling when we may need them again and need them badly.

The difficulty in estimating London, indeed, is that the decision must depend largely on history as yet unmade. Much that seems at present deplorable, absurd in itself and vicious in its tendency—his primitivism and his violence,— may turn out quite otherwise. Just now nothing seems worse than to encourage a general addiction to violence, and we hope no doubt never to have need of it. But no reader of *The Iron Heel* or of the daily papers can help fearing that the day may come when physical prowess and a capacity for violence will be a man's most valuable traits. If so, that day will see Jack London's final vindication.

[1938]

Steinbeck: Through a Glass Though Brightly

THE LONG VALLEY carries its reader back to Steinbeck's first published volume, *The Pastures of Heaven*. Here is the same beautiful countryside, with the same inhabitants—the half-wits, the delightful Mexican peasantry, the Americans who are either healthy normal farmers or interesting psychological freaks. It is true that in *The Long Valley* there are also vigilantes and Communists, to remind us that times change, but since Steinbeck is concerned not with external facts, but only with their odd states of mind when lynching or being lynched, they do not jar against the general tone of the picture. They take their place in the immemorial spectacle of the ill-fated race of men.

Surely no one writes lovelier stories, yielding a purer pleasure. Here are tragedy and suffering and violence, to be sure, but with all that is sharp and harsh distilled to a golden honey, ripe and mellow. Even cruelty and murder grow somehow pastoral, idyllic, seen through this amber light, as one might watch the struggles of fishes and water snakes in the depths of a mountain pool. Beyond question, Steinbeck has a magic alchemy, to take the sting out of reality and yet leave it all there except the sting. Perhaps it is partly the carefulness of his art, with endless pains devising and arranging every detail until all fits perfectly and is smooth and suave as polished ivory. But probably it is more the enchantment of his style, of that liquid melody which flows on and on until even such an experience as a man's dying of thirst in the morning sunlight among remote and rocky hills can seem not altogether ugly, because it has become a legendary thing that happened once upon a time.

Proper distance, I think, is the secret of this effect—to place people not too close nor too far away. In the middle distance they cannot touch us, and yet we can see their performances with the greatest clarity and fullness. Detachment, of course, is the essential: we are here to contemplate only, like the Lucretian gods but less remote. We feel the appropriate emotions—pity, sympathy, terror and horror even—but with the delightful sense that we are apart, in the audience, and that anyhow nothing can be done or needs to be done. Such a form of contemplation—which some would like to have the function of all art—is so agreeable, presumably, because it frees us from all responsibility. It is a tremendous relief to get rid of our ordinary burden of feeling implicated in human destinies. It is indeed for the moment to become a god, sitting in godlike isolation

> holding no form of creed,
> But contemplating all.

Such seems to me the attitude that is induced not only by Steinbeck's earliest and latest work, but by almost all of it, and that largely accounts for his popularity. *Tortilla Flat,* with its rococo comedy, ironic and romantic, ornate and mannered, may be a photographically accurate portrayal of the poor Mexicans of Monterey, but it leaves its readers amused and incredulous onlookers. Is *Of Mice and Men* an exception? It has more reality than *Tortilla Flat,* of course; its dialogue is extraordinarily lifelike and lively, as is most of Steinbeck's talk, for he is amazingly observant; but George and Lennie seem to me unbelievable—the flavor of grenadine is too strong. In any case, even if there have been half-wits as amiable as Lennie with friends as devoted as George, the question is not of reality, but of the attitude toward reality. Does anyone, in reading the book, participate in the fate of these men as their inevitable doom rolls upon them? Or does one watch merely, without sharing?

Steinbeck's reticence threatened to give way at least once: in his least successful novel, *To a God Unknown,* a strange and puzzling version of the Joseph story, full of myths and symbols and mystical identification with the earth. The hero, who is one with the processes of life in nature and men, finds himself comprehending all people so thoroughly that he can have relations with none. After his brother's murder, he says to his father's spirit:

Thomas and Burton [his other brothers] are allowed their likes and dislikes, only I am cut off. I am cut off. I can have neither good luck nor bad luck. I can have no knowledge of any good or bad. Even a pure true feeling of the difference between pleasure and pain is denied me. All things are one, and all a part of me. . . . Benjy is dead,

and I am neither glad nor sorry. There is no reason for it to me. It is
just so. I know now, my father, what you were—lonely beyond feeling loneliness, calm because you had no contact.

So might Steinbeck's reader, whether rightly or wrongly, be
tempted to speak to him. In *To a God Unknown* he seems
for once to commit himself to a point of view, of identification with everything and detachment from everybody.

A reader of the passage just quoted can hardly help thinking of Steinbeck's neighbor, Robinson Jeffers. As writers the
two have little in common, but they do share this detachment, and furthermore they also share a preoccupation with
physical suffering, cruelty, and violence. Are these two qualities related? When a man becomes too aloof from mankind,
so that the life of men turns for him into a mere aesthetic
spectacle to be exploited for its various notes and colors, does
his human nature revenge itself by forcing upon him an
obsession with power in its most repulsive forms? Is a surrender of humanity and an assumption of godhead likely to lead
to such a result? Only a psychologist could answer the questions; but perhaps one observation might be permitted to a
reader: that a taste for books which place one in the situation
of a superior being above the fever and the fret and apart
from one's fellows may be an undesirable taste. Apparently
many people reconcile themselves to being human only with
great difficulty and would much prefer to be almost anything
else—a mountain or a beast or a god—in order to escape the
limitations and troubles and obligations of humanity; but

the literature which encourages these impossible fancies may not be very good literature.

It will be objected that these are social and moral considerations. So they are—but nonetheless appropriate to literature, a social and moral art. But to take the aesthetic view, and to return to Steinbeck, it may be asked whether detachment is good for a writer's writing—or whether "detached" writing makes the best reading. To stand aside and contemplate these creatures with pity or with admiration—it is not so interesting as to get inside them and participate in their living. For one thing, the detachment is relatively monotonous, and leads to monotony—as well as to languor and softness, however seductive—of style. No first-rate novelist or playwright, I venture to say, has gone in for detachment or imposed it upon his readers, but quite the reverse: the best impose the most complete participation.

Steinbeck's finest work affords a case in point. *In Dubious Battle* tells of a fruit pickers' strike led by Communists. To be sure, one may surmise that the author speaks through the mouth of the doctor who sees little difference between men and microbes, who doesn't "want to put on the blinders of 'good' and 'bad', and limit" his vision, yet who wishes to give help to men who need it simply because they need it. But, however that may be, *In Dubious Battle* achieves an effect that none of Steinbeck's other books do: the reader does not stand by and look on; he lives through the strike, he shares it and takes part in it. To be sure, there are stiff and awkward passages of philosophizing, and the hero does not come out at all clearly; but these are minor blemishes. The strike and the strikers are directly and immediately conveyed, with none of the magic or the safety of distance.

In Dubious Battle is by all odds Steinbeck's best book because it is far and away the best written. Perhaps for once his material ran away with him; at any rate his style disappears into the material and they become indistinguishable. Here is none of that mellifluous and silky flow, of that saying that things were fierce and harsh and savage in the sweetest and most musical of words. The writing, sharp, energetic, and unnoticeable, follows and fits the stuff, and is worthy of it: more could hardly be said. For the story is the tragedy not of one but of many individuals—it is a national tragedy told through individuals. The theme is great, the execution excellent. And incidentally it has more sheer excitement than anything else of Steinbeck's. Yet the American public would have none of it. The public probably does not want to get too close to any reality that amounts to anything. It prefers rococo Mexicans and saccharine half-wits carefully kept in the middle distance.

It must be said, however, that *In Dubious Battle* now shares its excellence, though nothing else, with the series of four stories which conclude *The Long Valley*. These stories concern a little boy and his ponies, his parents, his grandfather, and the hired man. They are so well told it is hard to see how they could be better. Delicate and sure, they attain perfection in their kind. And here is no detachment, no distance. The writing is reserved and economical, but it leads straight into the characters and the relations between them. In this respect *The Red Pony* shows a gain over *In Dubious Battle,* in which necessarily the emphasis was upon external action. That *The Long Valley* should close so well is auspicious.

[1938]

The American Way

ANY TRAVELER in a mountainous country knows that, in trying to reach a high peak he sees on the distant horizon, he must be ready at any moment to change his course. An open grassy valley ahead looks inviting, but leads him among bogs and cliffs. Then, however reluctant, he has to turn aside—the sooner the better—and try another and probably less easy path.

The high goal which the American people set themselves still rises in the far distance. No one maintains that we have reached it, and few deny that the road we have followed has led us farther away from it than we were a hundred years ago and has landed us among appalling difficulties. It is time we asked ourselves whether we had not better try a new way, or perhaps even set ourselves a new and less arduous goal.

To the latter question I trust the answer will be an emphatic "No!" There is no need yet to give up hope of a country in which every person will have a fair chance to live, according to his own lights, the best life possible for him. "The American dream," James Truslow Adams calls this hope, "a dream of a social order in which each man and each woman shall be able to attain to the fullest stature of which they are innately capable." True as this statement may be, it might be more detailed, for Americans have had reasonably definite ideas as to the nature of this social order. Jefferson spoke for his countrymen when he singled out equality, freedom, and the pursuit of happiness as the keynotes of their political philosophy.

The phrase "created equal" has been too much laughed at. What Jefferson had in mind one can guess from the history of the doctrine of natural rights and the state of nature; what the phrase has meant to Americans is another matter. No one presumably has ever supposed that all men are born equal in all respects; the notion is too palpably false. Might not the traditional American belief be paraphrased thus: that all men ought to have, or are endowed by their Creator with, equal right to freedom in the pursuit of happiness? In other words, the many should not be sacrificed for the few, nor for that matter the few for the many; no one man ought to be sacrificed for any other. In this absolute sense, even though in no other, all men can be said to be of equal importance. Each man ought to be the judge of his own happiness, of what is best for him. For who can be trusted to judge of other people's welfare? No one is free enough from self-interest and class prejudice—not the politicians nor the clergy nor the scholars, nor certainly the rich. Not even the majority, although, since someone must rule, it had better be the majority, under such limitations and safeguards as can be invented. But, so far as is feasible in a body politic, let each citizen decide for himself wherein lies his well-being.

This principle may be easy to accept in theory, but it is

hard to carry out in practice. All of us are prone to think we
know how our fellow men ought to be spending their time
and their money, and what they ought to care about. The
man with two limousines and a chauffeur is outraged when
he hears that a laborer has bought a car instead of making a
payment on his mortgage. The laborer grows indignant over
the millionaire's private yacht. The millionaire's daughter
condemns the stenographer who spends her wages on silk
stockings and a permanent wave. The highbrow mourns over
those who like swing music and movies, and the preacher
disapproves of those who choose the golf links rather than
the church. These may be trivial instances, but they help
to show how difficult it is to live up to the doctrine that
all men have an equal right to freedom in pursuing their
happiness as they see fit—a doctrine which, translated into
the realms of politics and economics, has tremendous consequences.

Or rather, to speak more accurately, it would have tremendous consequences if it ever were translated into those
realms, because in them the efforts and desires of different
men most plainly clash and the struggle is fiercest. The
prospect of reconciliation may well look almost hopeless;
yet I think Americans need not despair, if they will realize
certain implications of the American principle. To begin
with, even though the goal we set ourselves when we de-
clared our independence should prove unattainable, as it
almost certainly will, that is no reason for not getting as

close to it as we can. Furthermore, the principle does not require that the struggle be entirely eliminated, but only that every man should have an equally fair chance in the struggle. Nor does it require that any man is to attain happiness, but only that he should have a chance in his own way to pursue it. It is not as if we were setting out to guarantee everybody's complete felicity; that would be a "dream" indeed. All we commit ourselves to—it is plenty, of course, but not necessarily fantastic and impossible—is the effort to create a more just social order, more just to every member, in which the farmer and the banker, the factory owner and the mechanic have equal rights to the pursuit of happiness— equal only, not absolute. That is to say, the restrictions placed upon one shall be no more onerous than those placed upon another; the external obstacles encountered by one shall be no more severe than those encountered by another; one shall be as free as another, though neither is by any means entirely free.

The principle obviously has its negative side and its limitations. It rules out at once any undertaking which by its very nature involves the sacrifice of other people's interests. Criminal pursuits are banned as a matter of course. In the political field, we have debarred the man who thought he would like to be absolute ruler, and we may find that this prohibition has to be extended also to the economic field. In fact, we may find that the liberties of many have to be further restricted in order that those of still more people may be enlarged, and that enterprises which heretofore have passed unquestioned need to be sharply scrutinized. But surely there are still enough ways of living and of making a living which enhance the common welfare to afford every man sufficient scope for his ambitions.

Such, then, has been the traditional American goal; the question which now faces the nation is whether it can best be approached by the road which we have followed in the past. First of all, we must recognize that the dream itself was conceived by an agrarian society, a loose, simple, open, free society of yeomen, artisans, and tradesmen, a rural world of farms and small towns. In such a world the condition of equal freedom and opportunity seemed not impossibly remote and the way thither not impossibly difficult. The chief obstacles looked like the artificial creations of law in remote times and foreign countries. Get rid of special privileges and abuses, such, for example, as entail and primogeniture and slavery; give every man political equality with the ballot; prevent the concentration of power in government or in finance; and let each person alone to work out his own salvation. After all, there was plenty of room for everybody, and if unfair powers and advantages of one over another could be prevented, a rough approximation to social justice might reasonably be expected.

The old American way might best be described as atomic individualism—if you like, call it rugged individualism. It grew out of two things: the economic independence that

characterized a society in which relatively few were entirely
dependent on wages and salaries, in which most men were
their own bosses; and the apparently unlimited vacant land
which surrounded that society. As long as the free land
lasted, so did the possibility of independence, the openness
of opportunity. The outcome of this situation was the American ethics, commonly known as the American spirit, the
ordinary American's admiration of self-reliance, independence, initiative, of the man who can take care of himself and
stand squarely on his own feet, alone, asking no favor of anybody, ready to look anyone in the eye as an equal. Such have
been the conditions of self-respect in this country; such still
is largely our moral heritage. Can we keep it?

More and more as the years have passed, the early American scheme of things has taken on the semblance of a
Golden Age, a Lost Paradise. Many efforts have been made
to return to it, of which perhaps the last serious one was the
LaFollette campaign of 1924. These facts should be a warning that this country never at any time reached the New
Jerusalem it set out for, and that indeed it has rather traveled
away from it. The "American way" is, accurately, not the
way we have ever followed, but the way we hoped, and failed,
to follow. Like the politicians, the nation has been forced to
be "Jeffersonian in talk, Hamiltonian in practice." Yet, unlike the politicians', its talk, I think, has always been better
than mere lip service. The truth is that America has wanted
to eat its cake and have it too. Jefferson, although he was

forced to surrender, saw plainly that the growth of industry and manufacturing would be fatal to his vision; but most Americans, less clearsighted, have welcomed the factory system and the Machine Age as progress and development. Few of us have been as honest about it as Hamilton was; even those who have profited most from the destruction of independence and equality have pretended loyalty to the American dream.

The majority, with whom this loyalty was not pretense, should ask themselves where our gift of unrestricted freedom to the individual has landed us. Too often this gift has turned out to be a charter to exploit the public. Letting men seek as they pleased what they thought to be their own happiness, with vast economic opportunities wide open on all sides, has proved equivalent to permitting them to engross power over their fellows and to restrict and control the lives of others. Such power, which could not exist in a simple agrarian society, has been made possible by the growth of industrialism, with its factories, its great corporations, its gigantic accumulations of capital on the one hand and of propertyless workers on the other. A way of life which seemed ideal to a set of loose rural communities has betrayed us in the conditions of a new age, which demands a new way.

Americans have not yet fully realized that free land and the frontier are gone, that the United States is an industrial nation, and that we are living now in an intricate, close and closed, corporate and collective society. They still think and feel and try to live as atomic—or rugged—individuals. The acutest need of the nation is that its citizens should wake up and start adapting themselves to the new conditions, and answering some of the questions which press upon us more and more critically. Shall we abandon in despair the historic goal we set ourselves? Surely there is no need, yet. Shall we put the clock back a hundred years or more? We would not if we could. Shall we continue doggedly in the way we have followed so far, even though it has not led us where we wished to go?

This choice is possible, and demands consideration. We cannot, to be sure, return to the loose organization of the early republic; our fortunes are too tightly enmeshed for that. But we can, if we like, continue the line we have taken from the Civil War to the present, or at any rate until 1932. Since in modern circumstances "every man for himself" is no longer a practicable policy, nowadays when men are let alone without social control and direction, they combine in their own interests and fight it out—too often literally—group against group and class against class. Such is the inevitable result of harboring individualist principles of action in a collective age. The clash between actual conditions and inherited thought and practice has already led to lawlessness and violence, and is likely to lead to worse. If our governments are going to say "a plague on both your houses" and wash their hands Pilate-fashion, or if they take the side against the interests of the commonalty, the end will be, not anarchy, though we may come close to that for a time, but, for the sake of order, a dictatorship. The end will be some sort of fascism, or, to use older words, of tyranny and despotism.

If these fears have any basis, our need of finding a new course is bitterly urgent. The change in direction may look drastic and difficult; it may require the sacrifice of many cherished habits of mind and behavior; *but whatever way leads best to the American goal is the American way.* I beg the reader's indulgence while I repeat my statement of that goal: to give every man a fair chance to live, according to his lights, the best life of which he is capable; to secure to every man an equal right to pursue his own happiness as he sees fit, so long as his way does not preclude the rights of others. The question which faces us all is how, if at all, such a goal can be sought in a corporate industrial society.

One thing sure is that it has to be sought, not each by himself, but by all together. The search must be a common undertaking; it demands a type of social consciousness in which Americans, because of their historic background, have been singularly lacking. Two of our favorite maxims will have to be forgotten: "You can't change human nature," and "Any system would work if you could reform individuals." As a matter of fact, nothing is more malleable than human nature, and the only way to reform individuals is through reforming the system. We are all of us largely creatures of society, and any important social variation remakes our

minds. It is true that individuals have first to be persuaded
that society needs changing, unless we merely drift with the
current; but each step taken in social alteration will make
the next step easier, because people's minds will be conditioned to it. Furthermore, everything does not depend on
the good will of individuals; there are already powerful social
forces at work in the right direction, and the individual can
ally himself with them, and through them greatly augment
his single efforts. Similarly, other favorite ideas and ways of
life will have to be reëxamined and revised before we see how
the spirit which Americans have treasured can receive expression through the refractory forms of modern life. In the end,
however, we may find that these intractable forms are less
obstacles than advantages and means for fuller realization.

First of all, we need to ask ourselves again what we mean
by *freedom,* and what kind of freedom is possible and desirable in the close-knit modern world. I think we should all
agree that an absolute freedom from all human ties and obligations is neither possible nor desirable. Indeed, the word
freedom means little until one inquires, "Free from what and
for what?" Would not the answer usually be that one seeks
for oneself and for others the liberty, to borrow Mr. J. T.
Adams' phrase, "to grow to fullest development as man and
woman"? But the implications of that phrase are not speedily
unraveled. Americans ought to agree, if they are true to their
past, that there is a large area in which complete freedom
should be granted to private and even public speech and ac-

tion, as guaranteed by the Bill of Rights, for instance, in religious and other matters. Elsewhere at present lies the debatable ground.

How then do men and women reach their fullest development? Is it not mainly through fulfilling as completely as possible their functions as members of society? If so, the freedom in demand ought to be that to function as well and as fully as possible—and, it might be added, to be suitably rewarded. Such seems to me the only conception of liberty consonant with such a world as that in which we live, in which all our destinies are so intricately linked. That is what we ought to be free *for*. But of such freedom most men and women have painfully, appallingly little. The commonest and most grievous restraint is of course poverty, to which I shall return in a moment. But there are other fetters scarcely less burdensome which have to be struck off first.

Most of these come from the fact that too many people have been granted and are still protected in the wrong kind of freedom: freedom to rule over and to exploit their fellows. Would anyone openly maintain that the pursuit of his own happiness required that he domineer over the lives of thousands? I doubt it; if such were his real desire, he would at least conceal it behind some pretense of general usefulness. Yet such is in harsh fact our present condition; for, with jobs no more numerous than they are, whoever controls a man's livelihood controls his life, and the man whose living depends on another's whim is in no sense free. The problem, then, is so to restrict and manage economic power that it shall not infringe but shall advance the rights of others; and I refuse to believe that even those whose power is so controlled would suffer as human beings. No man for his full growth needs to be a despot. A more plausible argument, however, is that some men function best, as the most valuable members of society, through the exercise of such power. And indeed somebody has to run things, and the most capable and efficient should do it; but need they be completely independent? Might they not be subject to the general welfare?

Clearly, if we are to pursue our goal of freedom, many of our laws and institutions must undergo drastic change, and none more so than those connected with property and with business. We can no longer allow a man to say, "My business is my own, and I can do what I like with it." We must see to it that what he does with it serves the common good. In other words, we have too long regarded the rights of ownership as primary and absolute; they should be recognized in law and in public opinion as secondary, dependent on social function, and valid only so long as a social function is served. Of the clothing factories of his day Thoreau said caustically, "The principal object is, not that mankind may be well and honestly clad, but, unquestionably, that the corporations may be enriched." We must recognize, and embody in our laws, the reverse order, so that profit and property will depend on making the proper service to mankind.

Furthermore, the rights of ownership must be so adjusted

as not to interfere with the desires of others to be as valuable
members as possible of the body politic. Many men nowadays would probably be glad to run their businesses more
truly to the general benefit if their competitors would let
them, but are forced by competition to debase their goods
and to deceive and cheat the public. Thus the wrong freedom
of some interferes with what ought to be the right freedom of
others, to the detriment of all. Again, some employers take
advantage of our existing property system to work against
the welfare not only of the public and of their rivals, but
especially of their employees. A policy hostile to labor means
a policy hostile to the rights of American citizens—rights that
ought to be embodied in law—to pursue what seems to them
their own happiness. Who can deny that the usual demands
of labor—shorter hours, better wages, the right to organize
and to share in the controlling power of industry—would
lead the workers to a completer development as persons and
as more fully functioning members of society? If leisure, in-
come, and self-direction contribute to the well-being of those
who now possess them, they ought to be equally beneficial
to others. The demands of labor are legitimate; they interfere,
not with any one else's proper freedom or happiness or social
functioning, but only with the wrongly granted and archaic
property "rights." That a worker should not have a legal interest in his job, that employees and public should not have
a legal interest in all considerable industries, is becoming pre-
posterous. That one man like Henry Ford should be in a

position by a single word to shut down a vast business, throwing thousands out of work and dislocating our whole economic machinery, is fantastic. Both employees and public should have a voice, perhaps even a ruling voice, in the control of industry.

Such a statement implies, no doubt, that the government should assume duties from which it has hitherto been exempted. And it is true that to achieve liberty in the modern world we need a new view of government. Traditionally, Americans have been inclined in theory to cling to the view that the less government the better, to reduce it, in fact, to the bare minimum of policing. To be sure, they have always been ready in practice to use it for their own specific purposes, but they have been reluctant to be used by it. They have thought of it as a power quite outside themselves, a "necessary evil," to be kept down unless it could be exploited; they have not utilized it as a positive instrument of the common will. Today, however, the need for such an instrument is so acute that it is hard to see how the older view can continue to prevail. Now that society has become not atomic but highly organized, the difficulties of social ordering and guidance cannot much longer be shirked. Nor should we necessarily fear the growth of a Leviathan state, if that term implies loss of popular freedom. I do not say we run no danger of building up a burdensome bureaucracy, but I do say that that danger can be guarded against, and that meanwhile our only possible implement for the regaining of the liberties we have lost through the growth of our economic system is the government. It is ours; it is ourselves in action, no more to be feared than ourselves. Our trouble comes from our being so unused to joining together for common action that we are foolishly wary of any exercise of the common will.

Together with our dread of a Leviathan state goes an equal dread of paternalism, lest the moral qualities we admire should be destroyed. And no doubt it is true that a government which took too much care of people would tend to make them soft, weak, and flabby. To ask, however, that the government be used as a means to secure a wider freedom for self-fulfillment through a fuller social functioning is not to ask it to be paternalistic. The sort of common action which is desirable need not injure the traits of character which we prize. Perhaps in a sense any coöperative effort may seem to involve a certain loss of independence and therefore of self-reliance; but when this effort is directed toward achieving a greater joint or common independence, no harm is done. Surely to act as a member of a group or a community does not impair one's self-reliance or self-respect—rather the reverse. It gives one a sense of counting for something, and a stronger sense of it than one can ever get alone.

Men who were in a position jointly to exercise more control over their work and their lives would hardly be weakened in their energy and their self-confidence. It is rather, in fact, the existing situation, in which some relatively few possess too unconditional a command over many more, that is likely to destroy the qualities we wish to preserve. In such a time as the present, if initiative and enterprise are to be developed at all they must be developed through collective activity. No one can now go off into the wilderness and be enterprising all by himself. But though the frontier is gone, the pioneer spirit of courage, boldness, initiative, and self-reliance can still find an outlet through social channels. The change need not even involve any loss in ruggedness, for the one kind of action demands as firm a will and as strong a resolution as the other.

The lesson Americans need most desperately to learn is to work together rather than apart. But the attitude of "each for himself by himself" is so deeply embedded in our consciousness that the change is difficult. The archetypal picture of the world as "the battle of life" is implanted in us from infancy, and anyone who inquired whether the world must unavoidably be a battlefield, a rough-and-tumble fight, would be suspected of effeminacy. No doubt human life, perhaps fortunately, will always be a good deal of a struggle—it is unlikely to get too easy in the foreseeable future—but one might wonder whether, with so many common enemies, men ought to devote themselves to fighting one another. The American picture, inherited from generations for whom it served a vital purpose conforming to fact, has become ill adjusted to actuality; today it is excessively and misleadingly individualistic. We need a basic picture which implies rather more coöperation.

Some such preconception underlies the fear of Americans lest too great security and ease might be a bad thing—not usually for themselves, but for other people. These fears seem somewhat premature, and—curiously—they are as a rule directed, not toward those who now possess the most security and ease, but toward those who have the least. Some of our fellow citizens are born to fully guaranteed security and complete ease without lifting a finger; but such privileges are dubious. The current demand for security is for another sort altogether—for the kind our grandfathers and great-grandfathers actually had: the knowledge that a man able and willing to work will find work to do, and that his reward will bear some proportion to his abilities. None but the idle rich claim an effortless security. If, as many economists say, the productive capacity of the United States is capable of yielding enough for all, it gets harder and harder to justify the fact that the opportunities of so many are so meager. Poverty, want, ignorance, and disease, though the rare genius may surmount them, are for most men effective barriers to the best possible performance of their functions as members of society. Every man ought to be secure to the extent of being certain to have a fair chance, and, if the economists are right, ought to be able to get a large enough portion of the general abundance to make the most of himself. How this potential plenty is to be distributed is a question for experts, though anyone ought to be able to make a few suggestions. The point at present is only that, if America is to persevere in the pursuit

of her original goal, if men are to be given equal rights to
freedom in the pursuit of happiness, we must acknowledge
that they should have security of opportunity and of adequate reward. To achieve such security for everyone is our
communal undertaking; everyone's help will be needed if
we are to succeed.

Such a society will have to be coöperative rather than individualistic. It will have to emphasize the performance of
social function far more than mere ownership. Precisely because it is coöperative it will afford the individual a better
means for complete development, for attaining his "fullest
possible stature," than did the individualism of the past. And
though coöperative, it will not destroy the values of competition, for emulation and rivalry are as keen when men work
together as when they work against one another. Though it
must severely limit the rights of property and reward service
to society rather than ownership, it will not, within the
bounds of justice, discourage acquisition; on the contrary, it
will open wider possibilities to all. Above all, it will enable
Americans to stand squarely together and look one another
straight in the eye.

If America is to follow the new American way—the only
way which now leads toward the goal—the first step will have
to be drastic and even fundamental social change. There may
be those who will call it revolutionary. Not a political revolution: our present form of government can be made, with
some reforms, to serve our purposes, though we must use it

differently and to different ends. But there is no blinking the
fact that the American way may lead through something
very close to a social revolution—let us do everything in our
power to make it a peaceful and orderly one. Let us also remember that our country was born in revolution, and that
our first and greatest state paper, our official announcement
to the world of our existence, proclaimed not only the right
but, on proper occasion, the duty of revolution. The spirit
which did not hesitate to call into being a new nation ought
not to shrink from the call to create a new society, ordered in
all its parts according to the principles which we avowed in
the beginning. Not until we shall have created such a society
shall we have a country which we can call a democracy without blushing.

[1936]

Aucassin in the Sierras

SHORTLY after sunrise we started north from Tuolumne
Meadows; it was noon when we stopped to camp. On
our right was a little lake, from the opposite shore of
which a semicircular cliff of granite, banked with snow at its
feet, rose higher than the Woolworth Building. From the lake
a brook ran off to the left across a grassy slope, dotted like
a park with shrubs and trees; a hundred yards or so away,
brook and park alike disappeared abruptly into the wooded
gorge of Conness Creek. Beside the brook and near the edge
of this ravine we found a spot sheltered by a great boulder;
after relieving the pack mule, Gabriel, of his load and tether-
ing him in a meadow, we built a little fireplace and began
to get lunch. At ten thousand feet above sea level, cooking
takes a long time, because water boils before it gets hot. We
spread out an army poncho for a tablecloth, and waited.
Almost directly above us stood the great peak of Mount
Conness. Away from it to the north, beyond and above the
empty space of the thousand-foot-deep canyon, stretched the
whole northern range of the Sierras, an inextricable jumble
of pinnacles and spires and domes—a panorama senseless and
sublime.

Most people, I think, look at mountains through the eyes
of the romantic poets, people even who know hardly more

of Wordsworth or of Byron than the names. They may never
have read the lines about
                              a sense sublime
        Of something far more deeply interfused . . .
        The author of my purest thoughts, the nurse,
        The guide, the guardian of my heart, and soul
        Of all my moral being,

yet they feel that somehow nature in general, and mountains
in particular, are uplifting and ennobling. Perhaps the feeling
is a residue from the days when Emerson toured the lyceums
and sowed transcendentalism beside every water tank on the
railroads. I do not believe that the idea is often examined or
brought to the test of experience. I doubt whether the majority, if they looked into the matter candidly, would find
after visiting nature that they had passed through a religious
experience or that their morals had undergone noticeable
improvement. No doubt they enjoy being out of doors—but
for other and less exalted reasons. Indeed, why should anyone
assume that mountains are peculiarly divine? They surely
stand, in that respect, on the same basis with the rest of creation; if "the firmament showeth His handiwork," so likewise does everything else. The notion which I question, and
which I think erroneous and even pernicious, is the very
common one that the Divinity avoids human society and
prefers the wilder fauna and flora to human beings. The
hermits of the early Middle Ages, who might be cited as
seekers of God in the wilderness, understood these matters
better than we: they did not, as a matter of fact, seek God

in the solitude, but rather went to the solitude in order that they might seek God in themselves. They were mystics, not romantics. They had none of the modern feeling for nature, and their religion was probably more advanced than our own—for there is something unpleasantly animistic in our attribution of divinity to rocks and trees.

I have never been able to share the common antipathy to hermits. I do not mean, of course, the mere misanthropes, or the nature lovers like Thoreau, who spend more time listening to bullfrogs and woodpeckers than to the still small voice; I mean the sort who fled the world in order to practice inward religious contemplation. One is told that such holy men would not be good citizens, but I question that statement. For one thing, there is more than one country to be a citizen of. Furthermore, I believe that a sprinkling of hermits might be highly beneficial to the United States. Out of our hundred million we could afford to spare a few hundreds who would make us ask ourselves questions and say to us: "The things you care for are valueless; your world is not only contemptible, but a positive nuisance; you know nothing of real happiness, and you are not on the way to learning anything about it." But, unluckily, there are no hermits in the Sierras. When modern men renounce the world, they do so for other motives than to lead the contemplative life. It was neither a mystic nor a romantic impulse that took us to Mount Conness. We did not feel that we were being illumined or ennobled; we were merely having a good time.

For three days we camped between the lake and the canyon. We enjoyed the rarest of luxuries on a hiking trip—leisure. Even after doing the innumerable chores which camping generates, we had time to spare—free time which we spent in going down a thousand feet to fish in Conness Creek, in going up two thousand feet to the top of Mount Conness, in lying on our backs and smoking, in admiring the scenery. I even thought, once in a while, of reading my book, which was Andrew Lang's translation of *Aucassin and Nicolete*. It was pleasant to realize that there was a book handy and that I did not want to read it.

Charming essays have been written on the advantages of outdoor reading, by people who say that they get the most pleasure from Thoreau in a pine grove or from Whitman by the seashore. They deceive themselves; there is nothing in this agreeable fancy. The best place to read is in a quiet room at night with the curtains drawn; then the outside world is least insistent and least likely to break in on the world of imagination. Nothing is clearer than that nature disapproves of reading: she does everything she can to make it impossible; she is always uncomfortable and always distracting. Conscious of her own shortcomings, she is jealous, like a poet's wife, of the more ideal mistress, and keeps nagging for one's whole attention. After all, books are unnatural; by them our minds, which were framed so that we might trap woolly elephants and elude saber-toothed tigers, are seduced into all sorts of impractical activities. If printing had

been invented twenty thousand years earlier, there would
probably be no human race today. Consequently, when
starting on an extended visit to nature, one had better leave
all one's books at home.

Yet I was glad that I took *Aucassin and Nicolete* to the
Sierras. An addict to the drug habit of reading is uncomfortable unless there is a book near by; *Aucassin* was too small to
be a nuisance, and I was familiar enough with it already not
to pay it any attention. Besides, I felt that the trip ought to
be good for Aucassin. I doubted whether that damoiseau,
so courteous and gentle and debonair, had ever done anything of the sort before. Not that he was a mollycoddle—he
was "hardy of his hands," and found no difficulty in defeat-
ing an entire army and capturing its leader; but both he and
Nicolete seem to have been almost blind to the charms of
nature. Perhaps it was because they were able to think of
nothing but each other. Aucassin once spurred his horse all
day through thickets of thorn and briar, until he could have
been trailed by the blood on the grass; "but so much he went
in thoughts of Nicolete, his lady sweet, that he felt no pain
nor torment." If he was as absorbed as all that, it is certain
that he gave little heed to the natural beauties of the forest.
Nicolete, to be sure, goes camping in the woods, but not by
choice—only because she prefers camping to being burned at
the stake: "Now the forest lay within two crossbow shots,
and the forest was of thirty leagues this way and that. Therein
also were wild beasts, and beast serpentine, and she feared

that if she entered there they would slay her. But anon she deemed that if men found her there they would hale her back into the town to burn her. . . . Nicolete made great moan . . . then commended herself to God, and anon fared till she came unto the forest." The lack of enthusiasm for nature is patent. To the modern reader, Nicolete's walk sounds charming, and so does her life in the little lodge she built of boughs and oak leaves and liles; but her sojourn in the forest is only one proof more of her devotion to Aucassin. No, I do not believe that even after they were married and were able to think of something besides each other, they spent their summers camping in the wilds of the Cevennes. In fact, it is easy to imagine their look of astonishment had anyone suggested such a pastime to them; and there is much to be said for their point of view. Why, indeed, should anyone spend his substance, time, and spirit in seeking remote discomforts—in order to sleep on hard, and bitter cold, terra firma, to eat cornmeal mush and beans and dried apples, to grow day by day stupider and stupider, and dirtier and dirtier? One gets close to nature—true; but there are some aspects of nature that I think the eulogists have overlooked. One, as I have intimated, is that she hates the human mind; she kills it at once, so that for weeks at a time a camper may go without using his brain above the medulla oblongata. Another is that nature—one would not have thought it necessary to scale mountains in order to discover this self-evident truth—nature is essentially dirt, dirt and nothing else,

dirt past, present, or future. Some of it at the moment in the
Sierras is in the agreeable forms of granite precipices, mari-
posa lilies, and wild deer, but so much of it is frankly dirt
that the camper soon returns outwardly to the clay of which
he was made. In short, any protracted, genuine association
with nature means a reversion to a state of brutal savagery.
Is that a thing for a rational creature to enjoy?

Aucassin certainly would have thought not, and another
member of our party would have agreed with him. Our mule,
Gabriel, plainly regarded the expedition with disapproval.
Gabriel was a revelation to me. I had supposed that I would
as lief travel with a leopard or hyena as with a mule, but
Gabriel convinced me that the mule has been slandered. It is
impossible to believe that any member of the species to
which he belonged could be malignant. Perhaps he was an
unusual mule; certainly he was very old, and older in mind
than in body. His was not a resistant green old age, nor had
he fallen into senile decay. There was no despair in Gabriel's
liquid eyes; he had got beyond despair, and passed from
resignation to indifference, with none of that protest against
fate by which the most hopeless creature commonly shows
a last flicker of the love of life. And because he had mastered fate, he mastered us. To speak harshly to him was
difficult, to think of striking him impossible. We traveled
therefore at his pace, which was all but invisible. What had
to be done, he would do without remonstrance, but he would
not pretend to like it. He was the only creature I have ever

heard of who had successfully attained the Stoic ideal of
ataraxy. Yet Gabriel did not spurn what alleviations life had
to offer. He derived unmistakable satisfaction from a kind of
knot grass with brown seeds, and he delighted in the flavor
of a fragile white flower on the order of the anemone.

If Gabriel seemed extraordinary to us, I daresay that nothing in him seemed so strange to us as our conception of
pleasure did to him. His attitude toward forests and mountains was medieval, like Aucassin's: they were highly dis-
agreeable. We, on the contrary, being good moderns for all
our understanding of the medieval point of view, reveled in
them. I shall not attempt to describe the Sierras; they always sound quite unreal, and a little foolish, like the scenery in Shelley's *Prometheus Unbound*—pendent crags of
rose-hued granite, lofty pines and fir trees that soar out of
sight, meads pied with myriad flowers, where one walks
through fields of wild cyclamen and sleeps on beds of white
violets. Besides, the task has been performed by the authors
of the railway folders. The Sierras might have been invented
to illustrate the prospectuses: "Rugged peaks stand sentinel
high above the clouds . . . great waterfalls sparkle among
the pines . . . here and there, tumbling brooks, whipped into
foam by their rocky beds, fling themselves over cascades or
beat against their imprisoning walls of rock . . . one finds
oneself amid the great gorges, confronted by titanic walls
of basalt and amazed by the giant summits that rear their
heads in clustered grandeur ten to fourteen thousand feet
above the sea."

The Sierras, obviously, have to be pictured in unrhymed
iambics, and only a composer of cinema captions can do them
justice. The prose style of Hollywood has been modeled on
their scenery. Nowhere is nature more natural; she has all
the grand simplicity of a Zane Grey hero. The advertisement
says with truth that those mountains are ideally suited to
"the average man or woman whose heart yearns to scale the
heights and penetrate the solitudes and appease his love for
the beauties of the great out-doors." However, even one who
is not an average person wasted by the unslaked ferocity
of his passion for nature need not be deterred by his comparative frigidity. Under the influence of the Sierras, he
will become natural as he has never been natural before.

Everyone knows, of course, that this sort of nature worship is an altogether modern sentiment. Medieval people
had no objection to being out of doors, provided they could
be perfectly comfortable; Aucassin did not insist on staying
in his castle:

> At Biaucaire below the tower
> Sat Aucassin, on an hour,
> Heard the bird and watched the flower.

But they had a decided preference for sitting in gardens
where the sunshine was warm. They had no liking for wildness. When one ponders it, the predilection for the primitive,
not invented till the eighteenth century, is an odd thing.
Perhaps the most comforting explanation of it is the common
one that we are overcivilized, that the last refinement of

sophistication is a taste for simplicity. The argument runs
as follows. In the heyday of Alexandria, Theocritus grew
homesick for the shepherd's life in Sicily; Horace fled, at
intervals, to his Sabine farm; within the last century the cult
of simplicity has had many devotees—whenever we can, we
flee from the complications and artifices of the feverish mode
of life we have made for ourselves, to a healthier and more
wholesome way of living. Really, it is a pleasant notion; it
shows that, however our vast cities might strike an unbiased
observer, we are still good at heart. But I fear that this idea has
little save its agreeableness to recommend it.

I can imagine too easily what Aucassin would say if one
explained to him the supercivilization of the twentieth century. His answer would run something like this: "Is the life
in your towns so overrefined that you need to seek relief?
Are your manners to one another so studied, so urbane
and formal, so artificially elegant—is your deportment so
minutely regulated with a view to the amenities, that the
restraint grows intolerable and you must flee to the desert?
I confess I should not have thought so. On the contrary,
in comparison with the life at the court of my father, Count
Garin de Biaucaire, your life and your behavior seem to me
rather too natural and simple, if not downright boorish and
brutal. Even the hinds and churls whom I met in the forest
during my search for Nicolete could teach manners to the
crowds which throng your streets. You have almost altogether
lost the art of conduct, as you have lost so many other arts

which once ameliorated existence. Surely you have small cause to foster a passion for the primitive; I can see no need of your striving to become less civilized than you are. Rather the reverse: you have lost the one great ideal which, whatever our shortcomings, we held firmly in the twelfth century— the ideal of the truly cultivated and accomplished man. What gain can be hoped from imitating untamed animals or un-couth men, from substituting what we call *vileinye* for the *curteisye* which was our high aim? Men can never become too civilized."

But to find a reply to Aucassin is not difficult. I grant at once that our manners are inferior to those of his Biaucaire. I grant that if one compares him with such modern heroes as Jack London's Sea-Wolf or Mr. Dreiser's Titan, or com-pares Nicolete with the heroines of *Flaming Youth* and *The Beautiful and Damned,* the progress of civilization begins to look very crablike. But Aucassin's Biaucaire exists only in a poem, and must differ widely from the France of actuality. I am not ready to concede that a comparison of Philip Augus-tus' subjects with President Coolidge's would result entirely in favor of the former. *Aucassin and Nicolete* presumably shows less what the twelfth century was than what it ad-mired. I cannot altogether sympathize with its taste; even with due allowance for Andrew Lang's translation, I feel that the extreme refinement and delicacy of twelfth-century taste is a little saccharine, a little rococo, with just a hint of some-thing meretricious verging on the tawdry. The men of the twelfth century, no doubt, had learned to desire the courtesy, grace, and elegance which they did not yet possess. They were plodding, so to speak, from Merovingia to Versailles. And when they finally reached Versailles, they were, as always, dissatisfied. Marie Antoinette liked to play at being a milkmaid, and lost her head in an explosion of savagery. It looks like merely the old, inevitable fallacy of the remote. Until they try it, men think that civilization will cure their ills; as soon as they try it, they think that natural simplicity, which is to say, savagery, will bring the remedy.

And yet, for all its plausibility, I hesitate to accept the statement that the modern addiction to nature proves our extreme sophistication. I think I detect a fundamental difference between the pastoral and bucolic diversions of Theocritus, Horace, and Marie Antoinette, and our own excursions into the primitive. The queen of Louis the Sixteenth would never have trudged after Gabriel all the way to Mount Conness. When we go camping, our mood is not that of courtiers dressed as Dresden shepherds at a *fête champêtre*. Our feeling is more akin, I fancy, to that of a Red Indian who has had to live for a time in civilization and who succeeds at last in escaping back to aboriginal life. It is a feeling of profound relief and release.

I speak without knowledge, but I suspect that camping is popular nowhere outside the United States. I am willing to hazard the suggestion that in our feeling for nature we differ somewhat from older countries. I attribute the fact (as everything is attributed nowadays) to our long Age of Pioneering, which began in 1607 with the landing at Jamestown and which is now just drawing to a close. For ten generations, large numbers of us have reverted to the most primitive conditions of living, as hunters, trappers, prospectors, homesteaders in log cabins and sod huts. Generation after generation has deliberately stepped down the scale and lived like savages in the wilderness. What is the effect of such retrogression? Most great migrations have been irruptions of barbarians into more highly civilized areas; we have reversed the process. The psychological results, I think we may assume, however much we admire the pioneers, cannot have been altogether salutary. A civilized man must lose something when he leaves civilization behind him. But however that may be, I suggest as one result of our Age of Pioneering the formation of our national hero cult. Consider the type of man to whom the American public pays not lip service but genuine respect: he is a man distinguished for physical prowess, endurance, courage, initiative, and a rudimentary sense of fair play—other moral qualities are secondary, and mental qualities, except an alertness like a wild beast's, are nowhere. It is obviously a pagan and a barbarous ideal; in fact, it is precisely the ideal which the Anglo-Saxons brought to England with them in the sixth century and embodied in *Beowulf.* It is the ideal set forth most sharply by Jack London: the man who can win in a fight is the "better man."

Well, there are worse types than the barbaric hero, the
viking—but I do not think we can call him civilized. What
I wish to point out is that, as our widespread reverence for
this type shows, many of us are at heart barbarians who have
had a terribly complicated and artificial civilization thrust
upon us suddenly. Among this number I should include all
those who truly like to go camping. We make a recreation
of what to our forefathers was bitter earnest. When we get
into the wilderness, we are reverting to type, and for a time
we rejoice like one who has come home from a strange land.
Man, it has been pointed out, is not a domesticated animal,
but the chief of the wild creatures, and perhaps Americans
are still a little wilder than some other nations. To say, however, that when my friend and I roamed over the Sierras we
were like tigers escaping from the zoo to the jungle would
be exaggerated and misleading. The tiger is glad to stay
in the jungle, but after a few weeks we were quite ready to
return to the fleshpots of civilization. And so it goes, both
with individuals and with the race: neither civilized nor wild
life proves altogether satisfactory. None of us nowadays
would hope for much from a romantic "return to nature,"
even were it possible. We know too well that Hobbes was
right when he called the natural life of man "nasty, poor,
brutish, and short." Nor, on the other hand, can we share
Aucassin's naïve faith in the virtue of civilization. We know
too well that any civilization made by human beings will
be imperfect to the point of abomination—until, that is, man

has become thoroughly domesticated, or, in other words, entirely tame. And somehow I cannot help being glad that that prospect is remote and improbable. I prefer endless cycles of varying discontent and failure.

After all, is perhaps Gabriel's solution the best: what will be, will be; since nothing matters, take quietly whatever comes and make the best of it? I am sure that Gabriel would have thought Dr. Johnson's saying as true for mule as for man: "Human life is everywhere a condition in which there is much to be endured and little to be enjoyed." Frankly, I must confess that I should not know how to answer Gabriel, nor have I ever met anyone who knew the answer. Perhaps, if we had found a hermit living alone in a cave when we went down to fish in Conness Creek, he might have been able to give us a better solution. Perhaps, indeed, we should all be wiser if it were possible for us to consult a hermit from time to time.

[1927]

Poetry and Morals

IN 1856 ONE JAMES C. MOFFAT wrote: "Art, in itself considered, is neither moral nor immoral. It belongs to an entirely separate class of things." In 1891 Oscar Wilde said in his *Intentions:* "The first condition of criticism is that the critic should be able to recognize that the sphere of Art and the sphere of Ethics are absolutely distinct and separate." These are but two unusually clear-cut expressions of an idea that has become almost an axiom of criticism—a dogma to question which is nowadays scarcely respectable. The contrary view—namely, that art and morality have some connection—is rarely found outside the followers of Anthony Comstock. The only reputable writer I know of who still maintains this discredited heresy is Mr. I. A. Richards, who has many cogent remarks to make on this as on other aspects of criticism.

Before I speak further of Mr. Richards' theories, however, let me quote what I consider the most vigorous statement of the orthodox view, from Mr. Spingarn's *The New Criticism:*

> To say that poetry, as poetry, is moral or immoral is as meaningless as to say that an equilateral triangle is moral and an isosceles triangle immoral, or to speak of the immorality of a musical chord or a Gothic arch. It is only conceivable in a world in which dinnertable conversation runs after this fashion: "This cauliflower would be good if it had only been prepared in accordance with international law." "Do you know why my cook's pastry is so good? Because he has never told a lie or seduced a woman."

This passage I choose because it contains most of the con-
fusions of thought which are the basis of the general conviction that poetry and morals have no relation. What that
relation is I have no hope of being able to state with com-
pleteness and precision; I shall be satisfied if I can show that
there is some relation, or, better, that there are many relations,
and if I can indicate where these relations are to be looked for.

Unfortunately, it is necessary to begin as usual with some
discussion of terms. The word "poetry" need make no trouble;
concerning it I will say only that in general it is better to
speak of poems than of poetry, as it is better to speak of works
of art than of art. "Morality," however, is a trickier term.
I most earnestly wish to make no assumptions as to what is
"true" morality, to leave my own ethical theories as much out
of the matter as possible; I hope that what I have to say will
hold, no matter what one's taste in poetry or one's moral ideas
may happen to be. Yet I must give warning that I exclude
one not uncommon use of the word "morality": by it I never
mean merely the behavior which has the conventional approval of society without question as to its value. For example:
when Mr. Mencken says, as he often does, that morality is
a noxious thing, he means that he disapproves of the behavior
to which the majority give a conventional approval—he says,
in brief, that morality is immoral. I do not use the word as
Mr. Mencken does, but I shall try to exclude no other use
of it. No matter what sort of person or kind of life a man
admires, cares for, attributes value to, poetry has for him its

moral aspects: that is my thesis. If he honestly believes that the best way to live is simply to conform to the demands of society, well and good—for him, works of art will have something to do with morals, and legitimately—and equally so whether he be stoic, epicurean, Roman Catholic, utilitarian, or what not. My only assumption, and I do not think it a large one, is that the most moral man is the best man, the most moral life the best life, at least for each individual in his peculiar situation. In other words, I do not and cannot separate the concept of morality from the concept of value, as Mr. Mencken and some others do.

I wish also, if I can, to avoid the pitfall into which in my opinion Mr. Richards has fallen in his *Principles of Literary Criticism*. I agree with him that poetry is intimately related to morals, but our agreement goes no further. Mr. Richards, being a psychologist and a scientist, bases his whole argument upon naturalistic metaphysics from which he deduces naturalistic ethics: "What is good or valuable, we have said, is the exercise of impulses and the satisfaction of their appetencies." For all I have to say to the contrary, Mr. Richards may be right; my point is only that one does not need to be a naturalist in order to see that art and ethics are connected. I have no concern at present with the truth of metaphysical beliefs. What I have to say is supposed to apply equally to idealist, realist, materialist, or any other -ist. My argument is based upon metaphysical no more than upon ethical presuppositions.

Now to return. "Art, in itself considered, is neither moral nor immoral." "To say that poetry, as poetry, is moral or immoral is ... meaningless." *In itself considered ... as poetry:* what do these phrases mean? They must, so far as I can see, mean that if a work of art be considered without reference either to creator or spectator—simply as it is in itself—it is outside the realm of morals. This truism, I fancy, no one who understands it will question. Michelangelo's "Night," if regarded as merely a block of marble in a certain shape, if disconnected from the experience of Michelangelo and also from the experience of the man who looks at it, is an inanimate object to which no one would think of attributing moral qualities or a moral nature. So likewise everyone will agree that the canvases or the plaster walls impregnated with pigments which we call paintings are nonmoral. It is difficult, extremely difficult, to consider statues and paintings "as such," "as they are in themselves," to hold them in this isolation in the mind, but it can be done, with effort, if anyone thinks it worth while.

But to do this with a poem is so difficult as to be all but impossible. What is a poem, "in itself considered"? An arrangement of black marks on paper? A series of vibrations in the air? A hard question, which I shall not try to answer, especially as it cannot be answered without making metaphysical assumptions. Let each answer it for himself; however diverse our answers, we shall all agree no doubt that a poem apart from its relation to human beings is nonmoral.

The only trouble that can arise here is that someone may make a statement of the sort that "Hamlet's mother is an immoral woman." Anyone who feels tempted to make such a remark should ask himself whether Gertrude exists, for a nonexistent woman is certainly nonmoral; and whether he does not really mean that Shakespeare was immoral when he imagined Gertrude, or that an actress is demoralized by playing the part, or that Gertrude has a bad effect on the audience, or that a real woman like Gertrude would be immoral. If such a moralist will gird himself to think of *Hamlet* only as the play exists in itself, he is likely to agree that the moral question is beside the mark.

I can foresee only one source of objection to the preceding. It is possible to maintain (and it may be true) that works of art exist not only as physical objects—stone, pigments and canvas, paper and ink, vibrations in the air—but also as what I can call only metaphysical entities. This view would hold, for instance, that in their own right, apart from the experience of any reader, Hamlet, Gertrude, and Claudius exist; and according to this view it might be said, therefore, that some, if not all poems, when considered only as such, have morality in them—as in *Hamlet* a son's moral obligation to avenge a father's murder is recognized. Because this point of view raises the most perplexing difficulties, and also because it is very rare, I wish to dismiss it as briefly as possible. Let us concede that according to it there would be a connection of some sort between morality and a poem as it is in itself; yet I doubt whether the upholders of this view would go so far as to call such metaphysical entities poems or the characters in poems moral or immoral. As I understand it, these metaphysical entities do not live, but merely exist, and so cannot be said to live rightly or wrongly.

Such offensive quibbling is necessary only because the whole argument for the separation of poetry and morals is based upon a flagrant confusion of thought, a confounding of the poem itself with its effects and relations. "Poetry, as poetry, is neither moral nor immoral . . . therefore the sphere of poetry and the sphere of ethics are absolutely distinct"; so runs the reasoning of these critics. But the sphere of poetry is by no means identical with poetry "in itself considered," and it is only the periphery of the sphere that is much worth talking about or that as a matter of fact is talked about. (Mr. Spingarn, for instance, in only one sentence of his essay speaks of poetry as poetry; otherwise he very sensibly busies himself with poetry as related to people. In this he is typical.)

With one further remark, we may leave poetry in itself considered and go on to more interesting matters. This remark is that to limit oneself to poetry as such is to eliminate all question of value. Only when related to its author or to a reader, possible or actual, does a poem possess value. Whether or not, when isolated from persons, it possesses excellence, may be debatable, but not value. For nothing has value save with reference to something alive; and when we are talking of works of art, I think we are safe in saying that they have value only with reference to human beings. The critic who sets out to consider a poem as such abjures thereby any attempt at valuation and restricts himself to description— description of the object only, since he also abjures description of the poem's relation to writer or reader. We may wish him luck and go on to the aspects of the poem which for most of us are far more interesting. Almost everyone likes a poem, if at all, because it tells him something about the poet or because it affords him an experience that he is glad to have.

Mr. Spingarn, as a matter of fact, except for his one sentence about "poetry, as poetry," is interested in the relation of poem to writer. In fact, he insists that every critic confine himself to this one aspect of poetry. He never tires of repeating that the only questions for the critic are these: "What has the writer proposed to himself to do? and how far has he succeeded in carrying out his own plan?" Mr. Spingarn makes the large assumption that a competent reader repeats almost exactly the experience, or some phase of the experience, of the poet—an assumption which seems to me quite unwarranted. However, if we can bring ourselves to concede that the reader's experience of a poem entitles him to make inferences concerning the poet's experiences, we may embark upon a consideration of the poem's relations to its maker—though always with the caveat that we are sailing in the very thin air of dubious surmise.

The poet's experiences may be divided into, first, the basic or initial experiences, such as Wordsworth's sight of the field

of daffodils, or of London from Westminster Bridge, and
second, the creative act, the writing of the poem. No doubt
the writer also as a rule reads over his own work, but as to
what then happens in his mind I think we know nothing—
certainly little or nothing from the poem itself—so that this
aspect of the matter may be dismissed. With most poems,
we cannot even make a guess at the basic experiences; when
we can do so, we may limit ourselves to describing the experiences in question, or we may attempt a valuation of the
experiences. Into either undertaking morality necessarily
enters. The poet's morality conditions his experiences: some
men, by their morality—that is, by what they take to be the
best mode of life, or take to be most worth living for—practically cut themselves off from the possibility of ever having
any experiences at all of the sort that lead to the writing of
poetry. And similarly a poet, if he adopts not transiently
but permanently the attitude expressed in the following
lines, has a scale of values which is bound to set narrow limits
to his experience:

> I live not in myself, but I become
> Portion of that around me; and to me
> High mountains are a feeling, but the hum
> Of human cities torture.

However, I suppose no one will deny that a poet's point of
view as to what is the best way of life, as to what experiences
are most worth having, affects the experiences which he
actually does have—no one will deny, in short, that at this

point the spheres of morals and of poetry overlap, and that therefore any description of these experiences must contain a moral element. And I trust it is even more obvious that, if we pass any judgment of value upon these experiences, there are then two moral elements—the poet's, and our own.

It is equally obvious that the creative act also has its moral side—and here I think it is enough to let Mr. Spingarn refute himself. When he disposes of the matter by asking: "Do you know why my cook's pastry is so good? Because he has never told a lie or seduced a woman," to my mind he answers himself. If I were to dine with Mr. Spingarn, my interest in his cook's morality would be intense: not as to the cook's verbal honesty or his sexual life, but perhaps as to his attitude toward homicide, and certainly as to his culinary morality. As Mr. Spingarn says himself—and his saying is as applicable to cooks as to poets—"The poet's only moral duty, as a poet, is to be true to his art, and to express his vision of reality as well as he can." In other words, the poet's only duty, as a poet, and, I should add, when composing poetry, is to do his best. Here again the spheres of poetry and of ethics intersect. The actual process of composition, like the basic or initial experiences which precede it, is conditioned by the poet's morality—both by his "artistic conscience" and in other ways.

From conception to completion, a poem is shaped by its writer's morals—I am not referring now to his "artistic conscience," not to his morals as a poet simply, but to his morals as a human being. The subjects which he chooses, or, to speak more accurately, which choose him—if one may legitimately use either expression (which I doubt)—are selected in accordance with a scale of moral values; the poet's preference for this experience rather than that, his notion of what was most worth while in life, had much to do with the conception of, say, "Corinna's Going a-Maying," "On First Looking into Chapman's Homer," and "Laus Veneris." And so throughout the writing, the whole process is colored by these same attitudes, even to the choice of epithet, as in the line

> Thou hast conquered, O *pale* Galilean.

Few people seem to realize how saturated in didacticism most poems are or to see that Herrick is as didactic as Whittier, that

> Gather ye rosebuds while ye may,
>   Old Time is still a-flying
> And this same flower that smiles to-day
>   Tomorrow will be dying

is as direct a moral teaching as

> Who may not strive, may yet fulfil
> The harder task of standing still,
>   And good but wished with God is done!

However, what I wish now to emphasize is not the explicit moral teaching of poets, common and extensive as that is, but rather the almost universal prevalence in poetry of implicit moral attitudes. It may be a fact of no interest or importance to the reader, but it seems to me an indubitable fact, that a poet's morality colors and must color and determine his work. I should think, therefore, that a critic like Mr. Spingarn, who wishes the reader to enter into the poet's mind by some imaginative process, would have to make allowance for some sort of entering into the poet's morality. Unless we can manage to sympathize at least for a time with Swinburne's moral attitude, I do not see how we can tell what the "Hymn to Proserpine" meant to Swinburne.

Mr. Spingarn concerns himself with the reader's experience of a poem only so far as it may be assumed to be an index to the poet's experiences; most critics, however—and I think properly—give their attention first of all to the experiences which a poem affords its readers. And it is here—in the relation of poem to reader—that we reach the crux of our question: Should the reader permit morality in any way to influence his reading of poetry or whatever judgments about it he may make?

First of all, it is necessary—if we can—to keep a clear distinction between the experience itself and the consequences of that experience. Since the consequences are more readily disposed of than the experience, let us take them first. To begin with, are there any consequences? Agreement is general that there are; I know of no proof, but neither do I know of anyone who has maintained that literature has no effect of any sort, that it does nothing whatever but pass the time. In fact, the tendency is rather to exaggerate the effects of poetry, to stress a crude sort of imitation which I suspect is seldom found in actuality, as that reading about Ulysses will

make boys run away to sea, or to stress another, less dubious,
influence to the effect that reading poetry makes one more
open to experiences like the poet's, makes one more alive and
responsive to certain types of beauty:

> For, don't you mark? we're made so that we love
> First when we see them painted, things we have passed
> Perhaps a hundred times nor cared to see.

However that may be, all we need is the concession that
poetry has some effects of some sort or other on its readers,
to ask whether these are moral effects. One's answer, perhaps,
will depend on one's own morality; yet I think few, after
reflection, will answer in the negative. For myself, I incline
to say that the chief effect upon those who read poetry is in
a strengthening of their preëxistent attitudes: a hedonist, because of his predilections, is likely to be attracted to and to
be affected by poetry which reinforces his hedonism—and so
likewise with a Platonist, a nature mystic, and so on. No doubt
the poetry often gives a development, an enrichment, and a
refinement to the tendencies already present; and sometimes,
probably, a poet may be so persuasive as to alter a reader's
fundamental bias. In any case, if it be that the alteration is
either for better or worse, and not indifferent or negligible,
it is a moral change.

From Plato and Aristotle to Sidney, Shelley, and Mr.
Richards few theorists have ignored the effects of reading
poetry, and none that I know of have denied them. One of
the most emphatic and curious champions of the moral in-

fluence of poetry is Oscar Wilde, who paraphrases Aristotle
with approval, thus:

> To have a capacity for a passion and not to realise it, is to make
> oneself incomplete and limited. The mimic spectacle of life that
> Tragedy affords cleanses the bosom of much "perilous stuff," and
> by presenting high and worthy objects for the exercise of the emo-
> tions purifies and spiritualises the man; nay, not merely does it
> spiritualise him, but it initiates him also into noble feelings of which
> he might else have known nothing.

Yet Wilde, who devotes most of "The Decay of Lying" to
the thesis that "Life imitates Art far more than Art imitates
Life," also says that "The sphere of Art and the sphere of
Ethics are absolutely distinct and separate!"

At this point, I daresay, any lover of poetry is sure to be
ready with an objection of some violence. "It may be true,"
I imagine him saying, "that the reading of poetry has after-
effects and that if the poetry is good these also are good; but
is not there something almost indecent in this point of view?
Think of a man reading *Romeo and Juliet* with one eye all
the while on himself, thinking 'How good this is going to
be for me!' Surely, at the least while we are reading, we must
forget these future consequences and read the poem for its
own sake only; otherwise, it is impossible ever really to read
a poem at all. The first requisite is that one must care for
poetry for its own sake, and if one does, the talk about its
effects is impertinent or worse." I heartily assent, and apolo-
gize for having introduced the topic of results, which I

mentioned only because many eminent men had set a bad example. I gladly return to the question I asked some time ago: Should the reader permit morality to influence his reading of a poem or whatever judgments he may make about it? As to the experience itself, apart from valuation of it, I fear we cannot help ourselves; our basic attitudes, from which our tastes and preferences arise, are bound to play a part in our reading. I do not see, for instance, how a man to whom the pleasures of the senses are indifferent or obnoxious can greatly enjoy "The Eve of St. Agnes," nor how a thorough Buddhist can care much for Herrick or for any poet who loves the "veil of illusion." Furthermore, there are people who set no store by any experiences apart from results, who never delight in an experience for its own sake; such people condemn poetry as a waste of time, being themselves cut off by their moral code from ever knowing what a poem is. We can scarcely deny that our morality to some extent conditions our poetic experience.

We must also admit, then, that since the experience itself is thus conditioned, so also is our judgment as to the value of that experience bound to be. Here we arrive at the point which is focal for the criticism of poetry: the judgment which the reader forms as to the value or values of the experience afforded him by a poem. Actually it is this judgment which most of those who insist on the absolute separation of poetry and morals have in mind. They say that they are talking of poetry considered as such or as it is in itself, or that the two spheres are utterly distinct, but what they usually seem to mean is that the values inherent in the experience of poetry are not moral, but aesthetic, values. "Perhaps," they might admit, "a poet's life is influenced by his moral views, and since many poets express their points of view when they write, their poems also may contain their moral views in explicit or implicit form. And it may be that, since we are all fallible beings, we cannot help as readers being biased a little by our moral prejudices. Yet that after all is but a human frailty to be discounted as much as possible. When all is said, the fact still remains that what we care for in poetry is beauty, not morals. If a poem is beautiful and gives aesthetic pleasure, every sensible person pays as little attention as possible to these ethical considerations. Poems—or rather experiences of poems—must be judged, if at all, in accordance with aesthetic, not moral, standards. That is the only real point at issue."

I agree that that is the point, and I wish to meet it squarely. But "aesthetics," "beauty," and "morals" are all mischievous terms and had better be forgotten for a time, while we think only of that familiar experience, reading a poem. I shall attempt no analysis of such an experience; that is a psychologist's task, and has been admirably performed by Mr. Richards in *Principles of Literary Criticism* and *Science and Poetry*. In fact, I am less concerned with the experience itself than with valuations of it, especially with judgments of the simplest type, of the type which readers of poetry are constantly making—judgments quite noncommittal as to particular aesthetic or moral views, such as "I like this poem immensely," or "I don't care much for that poem." These may be restated in more cumbrous form as follows: "The one poem yields me an experience which I judge to be valuable for its own sake, and the other does not; the one experience I am glad to have had simply on its own account, and the other I should gladly have missed. The former was time well spent; without it my life would be poorer and I should be a poorer man. While I was reading the first poem, I was doing something which it was right and good for me to be doing. To read the second poem was a mistake." But to spend one's time well—is not that to live rightly and as one ought? and is not how best to live a moral question—indeed, *the* question of ethics? To be sure, in judgments concerning the values inherent in an experience, those values may be aesthetic, not moral; but the conclusion seems to me inescapable that every such judgment has a moral aspect, inasmuch as it is a decision concerning the best living of life.

Let me take a more specific example, the most unfavorable to my theory that I can think of: a man, let us say, whom we may call an extreme aesthete, who holds that the value of a poem is not in its "meaning" but in its "form," that a poem is like a Persian rug, valuable only for its color and design. On these grounds he prefers Austin Dobson to Shakespeare, because the former was a thorough artist and the latter was not. Is this man making an ethical as well as an aesthetic judgment? He is implying, at any rate, that a good way to spend one's time is in the contemplation of perfect forms. Or—if he should protest that he has no concern with values, that he gets the most pleasure from those poems most perfect in design, sound, and imagery, and therefore likes them best, but that he sees no reason for associating pleasure (or anything else) with value—should we not still be justified in maintaining that although he has refused to formulate an ethical code, nevertheless there is implicit in his conduct an attitude which has its moral aspect, that his preferences imply moral choices? Willy-nilly, he must decide to spend his time in this or in that way, and when he takes *Ballades in Blue China* from the shelf rather than *King Lear* his act inevitably indicates not only an aesthetic taste but also a moral decision. His poetic standards, which he must have though he refuse to confess to them, are connected with moral standards still—because, if I may repeat, every judgment, even if an unconscious judgment, of inherent value concerning an experience has its moral implications. All human experiences of any moment, together with their inherent values of whatever sort, are subject to moral valuation, and there is no reason for exempting aesthetic or, specifically, poetic experiences and values from this rule.

Perhaps a few possible misconceptions can be avoided at this point. Most of the connections which I have pointed out between poetry and morals seem to me relatively unimportant and uninteresting. I do not think the poet's morality as it appears directly or indirectly in his poem a matter of

much consequence, save as it may affect his "artistic conscience." I grant that a reader of poetry should lay aside his
moral theories so far as possible when he begins to read. Nor
do I ask that poems be esteemed for their after-effects in the
molding of character. Least of all do I wish to confound
aesthetic with ethical canons, though I cannot admit their
absolute separation, or to seem, in my effort to show that the
spheres of poetry and morals are not utterly distinct, to deny
that poems have innumerable nonmoral aspects and values
of the utmost importance. Yet I insist that a judgment
concerning poetic values is incidentally a moral judgment.
("Poetic values" is shorthand for "the values inherent in the
experience afforded by a poem.") To that extent poetic values
are bound up with, though certainly not identical with, moral
values. Mr. Richards goes too far when he says: "The world
of poetry has in no sense any different reality from the rest
of the world and it has no special laws and no otherworldly
peculiarities. It is made up of experiences of exactly the same
kinds as those that come to us in other ways." In part these
statements are open to question, and in part I think demon-
strably false. "The world of poetry" and "different reality" are
dubious and ambiguous expressions. And there seems to be
at least one element in poetic experiences which is peculiar
to them and *not* found in experiences which come to us in
other ways, the element contributed by rhythmical language.
Therefore I think that poetic values are different from other
values and can be considered as a class by themselves—which

Mr. Richards seems to deny. Yet they are after all one class of values, and morality, the business of which is to arrange classes of value in a scale, must deal with them. And not only so, but morality has every right, within the class of poetic values, to set up its scale also.

Some specific examples may make my contention plainer. In my opinion, "La Belle Dame sans Merci" is a poem singularly free from any sort of ethical implication and most unlikely in any way to involve the reader's moral views; also, I think it a poem of very great value. On the other hand, for me "A Psalm of Life" has little value, though replete with morals. Reading "La Belle Dame sans Merci" therefore would go in the list of things I think worth doing, and reading "A Psalm of Life" would not. Or, say that in general I find much value in Keats and little in Longfellow; then I should be foolish, other things being equal, to spend more time reading Longfellow than Keats—and to be foolish when we need not be is wrong. Or suppose that on some day in France I have to choose between visiting a Romanesque church and a seventeenth-century chateau; if I know that Romanesque churches usually give me something I care for and that seventeenth-century chateaux do not, I should probably be foolish and doing wrong to visit the chateau. At any rate, I have made a moral choice and formed a moral judgment about the value of architectural experiences—though I should hesitate to call either the church or the chateau moral or immoral in itself.

Seldom is there occasion to call a poem either moral or
immoral. Sometimes, however, for the sake of convenience
and brevity, there is no great harm in saying simply that a
poem which affords a valuable experience is a moral poem,
and that it is moral in proportion to the value of the experience it affords—or in saying still more simply that any good
poem is a moral poem. Or, to alter the statement a little, a
good poem is one which a moral man cares for—for, if the
poem is really good and the man does not like it, there is
something the matter with him and he is to that extent
imperfect. Good poetry, however, curiously happens to be
less interesting in this connection than bad poetry. One is
tempted at first to say only that a poem which yields a valueless experience is bad. I think, however, that a valueless poem
is neither good nor bad, but merely negligible. A bad poem
is rather one the experience of which it positively deleterious.
Yet a poem, I suspect, never harms anyone who does not like
it—such a one is repelled, annoyed, disgusted, and therefore
immune. The harm comes only when the reader makes a
false attribution of value, when he ascribes value to an experience he would be better off without. What happens I take
to be this: such a reader, having in himself incorrect attitudes
and a false scale of values, enjoys those poems which fortify
him in his undesirable condition. It is my belief, for instance,
that an adult of sound mind who delights in such poems as
"The Barefoot Boy" and "The Village Blacksmith" is too
infantile to be considered a good man; I call such poems

immoral because they tend to fix that infantility. If the reader disagrees, he can easily substitute examples which fit his own scale of values. The point is only that, whatever one's scale may be, all bad poems are immoral because they give aid and comfort to immoral people—people whose scale of values is false—and that anyone who likes bad poetry is to some extent immoral.

In the hope of showing that, no matter what one's aesthetics or one's ethics, the two are unavoidably related at many points, I have reduced the question of poetry and morals to its lowest common elements. If I have convincingly indicated even one point of contact, I have succeeded in my undertaking, for I have wished to show merely that they are related rather than to explain *how* they are related. Needless to say, a complete analysis and statement of these relations would have to be long and complicated, and could not be undertaken without the exposition of moral and poetic theories which I have now no intention of setting forth. Suffice it to state my belief that an accurate and complete treatment of the theme would develop far more numerous and intricate interrelations than those I have mentioned in this elementary discussion. I admit that these relations would be almost impossible to describe in full; but I protest that that is no reason for denying that they exist.

From the fact that no one, even with the best will in the world, has yet succeeded in separating poetry and morals, I conclude that they are inseparable. The more one ponders the matter, the more one wonders why the effort was ever made. Since God has joined them, why try to put them asunder? Mr. Richards traces the enterprise to its source in Kant and his alignment of the Good, the True, and the Beautiful with the distinct faculties of Will, Thought, and Feeling. The popularity of the attempt, however, is probably due to causes less exalted than transcendental philosophy, and has more to do with Victoria and Louis Philippe, with "young persons" and *jeunes filles,* than with Kant. As we all know, many stupid people within the last century have attacked as immoral and tried to supress all art and literature which they thought not conducive to conventional behavior; their bad morality led them into bad aesthetics. In consequence, many would-be friends of the arts made the mistake of proclaiming that art had nothing to do with morality, when they should have attacked the low moral state of their opponents. Anthony Comstock should have been assailed not as an unsound aesthetician but as an extremely immoral man. But the defenders of art unfortunately accepted the bad morality without criticism as true morality, and so in turn they too were led into false aesthetics. The whole quarrel could arise only when both aesthetics and morals were in a singularly debased condition. Mr. Spingarn, for instance—I take him only as a sample—seems to have a conception of morals, so far as he discloses it, of a decidedly juvenile sort, as having something to do with telling lies and committing adultery, but nothing to do with professional honor. Disputants on both sides, having at the start taken for granted a conflict, have let their zeal rush them into battle half-armed, bad moralists without aesthetics, and bad aesthetes without ethics. After all, there is no good reason why either beauty or morality should be thought of as a nuisance, and anyone who will take the trouble sincerely to define the two terms to his own satisfaction will find not only that they are not hostile, but that they have much to do with each other. All the trouble comes from leaving either concept in a crude, unexamined, undeveloped condition.

[1929]

Sense Perceptions and Images

Sister, it is not earthly . . . How it glides
Under the leaves! how on its head there burns
A light, like a green star, whose emerald beams
Are twined with its fair hair! how, as it moves,
The splendor drops in flakes upon the grass!
Knowest thou it?
—SHELLEY

AT HALF PAST FIVE or six on Saturday morning, July 31, 1802, Wordsworth and his sister climbed upon the Dover coach at Charing Cross and soon rolled across Westminster Bridge on their way to France. The day was fair and at that hour the city was silent; upon the river were many small boats, and the countless buildings of London, with St. Paul's standing up among them, were unobscured by the usual cloud of smoke. Both travelers were struck with the unwonted aspect of the scene, the beauty of which Dorothy described in her journal; William indeed was so deeply moved that, sitting on the roof while the coach rocked along through Kent, he recorded the morning's experience in a sonnet, a moment's monument.

The month of August the Wordsworths spent at Calais with Annette and Caroline. In the late afternoon they often walked on the beach, looking at the distant English cliffs with their two lighthouses, listening to the waves, watch-

ing for the evening star and its reflections on the water.
Again Dorothy described the scene in her journal, and again
William was impelled to record one of these evenings in a
sonnet—an evening which seemed to him a holy time breath-
less with adoration.

Few of humanity's moments have been so completely
fixed and made lasting as these two. Not often do poets give
this privilege of living through and sharing with them the
particular instants out of which their poetry grows. As a rule
the basic experiences have been so dissolved before they re-
crystallize as the poem that they are lost beyond guess. But
in these two sonnets Wordsworth has shown how at least one
poet saw the world about him. Whether he saw it differently
from other men is not easy to say. I see no sign, for example,
that Wordsworth had more than most men what he himself
termed the first of the powers requisite to the poet, "an ability
to observe with accuracy things as they are in themselves."
Nor did these two scenes rouse more powerful feelings in
him than similar scenes have often roused in men who were
not poets; in fact, Dorothy was as *alive* as William to the
beauty of the scenes, but it may be that she did not feel a
kind of strangeness, a mysterious blend of majesty and holiness and calm which had for him an almost magical effect—
and which for him gave those moments a poetic value.

Wordsworth himself would undoubtedly have attributed
that value to the working of the power inadequately called
by the name of imagination. He would have said that to the

scenes his imagination gave a coloring or heightening. He might have added—for it was a favorite idea of his—that in this imaginative process he was detecting in the world something akin to his own mind, or the mind of man. Or he might have averred, as he often did, that he was half creating what he seemed to see—that he was imputing to the world something which was not there, but only in himself.

Once when Wordsworth was a schoolboy on his way home for vacation he spent a night at Patterdale. After dark he explored the shore of Ullswater and found a boat, which he took without permission. He rowed vigorously out upon the lake, keeping his eyes fixed on Stybarrow Crag, and as he drew farther from the shore he began to catch sight of the higher Black Crag behind Stybarrow. Then came to him one of his unforgettable moments:

> from behind that craggy steep till then
> The horizon's bound, a huge peak, black and huge,
> As if with voluntary power instinct
> Upreared its head. I struck and struck again,
> And growing still in stature the grim shape
> Towered up between me and the stars, and still,
> For so it seemed, with purpose of its own
> And measured motion like a living thing,
> Strode after me. With trembling hands I turned,
> And through the silent water stole my way
> Back to the covert of the willow tree.

So far the passage, like many others, shows only how the child or the poet is habitually constrained either to perceive

human "volitions and passions as manifested in the goings-on
of the Universe" or is "habitually impelled to create them
where he does not find them." The frightened boy alone at
night on the surface of Ullswater was in no mood to reflect
that as one's angle of vision lessens more distant objects become more conspicuous in the landscape, or that a mountain
was unlikely to assume the duty of avenging a stolen boat.
That grim shape, black and huge, striding after him with
measured motion—what was it? Surely not a natural object,
but something more than natural, strange and mysterious,
awe-inspiring as in later life he found the majestic city sleeping in sunlight and girdled with flowing water, or the tran-
quil heaven in the holiness of worship brooding over the
mighty being of the fluctuating sea.

The terror on Ullswater had an aftermath more extraordinary than the experience itself.

in her mooring-place I left my bark,—
And through the meadows homeward went, in grave
And serious mood; but after I had seen
That spectacle, for many days, my brain
Worked with a dim and undetermined sense
Of unknown modes of being; o'er my thoughts
There hung a darkness, call it solitude
Or blank desertion. No familiar shapes
Remained, no pleasant images of trees,
Of sea or sky, no colours of green fields;
But huge and mighty forms, that do not live
Like living men, moved slowly through the mind
By day, and were a trouble to my dreams.

Wordsworth was haunted for days and nights—by his recollection of Black Crag? His words do not sound so. The huge and mighty forms, he says, according to one version, did not live like living men; according to another, moved slowly, like living men, through his mind. However one punctuates the passage, whether

> ... mighty forms that do not live,
> Like living men moved slowly through the mind ...

or, as in the common version which I prefer,

> ... mighty forms, that do not live
> Like living men, moved slowly ...

in either case he compares and contrasts these forms, not with mountains, but with *men:* in other words, he was long troubled, awake and asleep, not by a memory of hills and mountains, of Stybarrow and Black Crag, but by dread unhuman shapes—yet the same shapes, presumably, which had frightened him on Ullswater, and which he had then connected with the ominous Black Crag.

In an enlightening note Mr. de Selincourt refers to this passage of *The Prelude.* The note concerns the passage on nature's influence in forming character which finally became

> Dust as we are, the immortal spirit grows
> Like harmony in music; there is a dark
> Inscrutable workmanship that reconciles
> Discordant elements. ....

In 1799 Wordsworth had first written:

> The mind of man is fashioned and built up
> Even as a strain of music: I believe
> That there are Spirits which, when they would form
> A favored being, from his very dawn
> Of infancy do open out the clouds
> As at the touch of lightning, seeking him
> With gentle visitations, quiet Powers! . . .
> With me though rarely in my boyish days
> They communed; others too there are who use
> Yet haply aiming at the self-same end
> Severer interventions, ministry
> More palpable, and of their school was I.
> They guided me: one evening led by them . . .

and then follows the account of the adventure with the stolen boat. Even so early as 1805 Wordsworth had eliminated the spirits and substituted Nature. Mr. de Selincourt comments: "When Wordsworth began to write *The Prelude* he still delighted to conceive of Nature not merely as the expression of one divine spirit, but as in its several parts animated by individual spirits who had, like human beings, an independent life and power of action. This was obviously his firm belief in the primitive paganism of his boyhood, and long after he had given up definite belief in it, he cherished it as more than mere poetic fancy." For example, this belief has left traces even in the final version of the lines

> Ye Presences of Nature in the sky
> And on the earth! Ye Visions of the hills!
> And Souls of lonely places!

instead of which in 1799 he had written the more specific

> Ye Powers of earth, ye genii of the Springs
> And ye that have your voices in the clouds
> And ye that are familiars of the Lakes
> And standing pools—

In Mr. de Selincourt's view, then, the schoolboy Wordsworth attributed his fright to the spirits which inhabit the mountains—and presumably it was these spirits that he could not forget for many days and that kept appearing in his dreams.

In later life Wordsworth tried to reconcile his boyish primitive animism with his reason by reducing the spirits to one and calling that one God. Whether there is gain in rationality is open to question; but there is no doubt that the change tended to obscure the original and essential nature of Wordsworth's most typical poetic experiences. In 1799 when he wrote the first passages of *The Prelude* he was still willing and able to tell the truth about his youthful perceptions, to tell how he had often had a sense that unhuman beings, at times half seen, half heard, were present, how in childhood he had more than once caught a glimpse of old Proteus rising from the sea. But in later years, partly because he did not wish the supreme moments of his life to be dismissed as mere poetic fancy, partly perhaps because he disliked conventional personifications of natural objects, but more because he quite rightly desired to think out a reasonable philosophy of life, he submitted his experiences to the criticism of common sense and rationality and orthodox piety. Moreover, as he frequently laments and as his writing bears witness, the experiences themselves ceased in early middle age. The result of the whole process, as embodied in the several versions of *The Prelude,* is that Wordsworth progressively obscured, confused, and falsified the character of his poetic experiences when those were open to the sorts of criticism which I have mentioned. On the other hand, not all his experiences, fortunately, seemed to Wordsworth to invite these objections, and them he has recorded with less modification.

While at Cambridge Wordsworth was in the habit on winter nights of frequenting the college groves. Among them stood one tree the memory of which never left him, an ash over the trunk and main branches of which ivy had grown in clusters, while all the twigs were hung with yellow tassels, bright against the glossy green, that trembled and shook in the breeze. "Often," Wordsworth says,

> often have I stood
> Foot-bound uplooking at this lovely tree
> Beneath a frosty moon;

but the fascination of the tree was not only, not chiefly, its physical loveliness, but its effect on Wordsworth's imagination:

> scarcely Spenser's self
> Could have more tranquil visions in his youth,
> Or could more bright appearances create
> Of human forms with superhuman powers,
> Than I beheld.

So read the lines in the 1850 version; in 1805 the "bright appearances" were *seen*, not *created*, and I have no doubt that the earlier word is the more accurate, though both words are needed for an understanding of what took place. Is it too much to believe that Wordsworth means here what his words signify, namely, that as he stood beneath this fantastic tree in the frosty moonlight he *saw visions?*—not that the tree made him think of elves or fairies or other traditional creatures of folklore, but that he *saw,* with his mind's eye but perhaps as visible as with his physical eye, "bright appearances"?

On at least one occasion, some years later than the time at Cambridge, the visions of the mind's eye, if we are to believe Wordsworth, became far more visible to him than the material world—so vivid, indeed, that the latter was obliterated. He wandered alone for three days through the solitude of Salisbury Plain and the southern downs, happening upon many relics of the Druids: then

> While through those vestiges of ancient times
> I ranged, and by the solitude overcome,
> I had a reverie and saw the past—

or, as the second version has it,

> from the solitude proceeded
> A reverie, and I beheld the past—

or, according to the final version,

> I saw
> Our dim ancestral past in vision clear.

In this vision or reverie he

> Saw multitudes of men, and, here and there,
> A single Briton clothed in wolf-skin vest,
> With shield and stone-axe, stride across the wold;
> The voice of spears was heard, the rattling spear
> Shaken by arms of mighty bone, in strength,
> Long mouldered, of barbaric majesty.
> I called on Darkness—but before the word
> Was uttered, midnight darkness seemed to take
> All objects from my sight; and lo! again
> The Desert visible by dismal flames!
> It is the sacrificial altar, fed
> With living men—

And again:

> —Gently was I charmed
> Into a waking dream, a reverie
> That, with believing eyes, where'er I turned,
> Beheld long-bearded teachers, with white wands
> Uplifted, pointing to the starry sky,
> Alternately, and plain below, while breath
> Of music swayed their motions. . . .

I quote the passage at some length because it contains the most detailed account we have of Wordsworth's visions. There is no difficulty here in tracing the processes of the poet's mind: prepared by solitude, which always assists to such experiences, he saw as it seemed outside himself the pictures with which the lonely place was associated; that is, because of the region's associations, the scenes through which he was passing awoke in his mind certain images, ancestral in kind, so vivid that they competed successfully with the physical ob-

jects about him, now blending with them, and now usurping
their place. Wordsworth for this once did what Bunyan is
said to have done habitually: "He looked on that which was
passing through his own mind and heart as though it were
something external"; Wordsworth did what Blake affirmed
was his own habit: "I assert for myself that I do not behold
the outward creation, and that it is to me hindrance and not
action. 'What', it will be questioned, 'when the sun rises do
you not see a round disc of fire something like a guinea?'
Oh! no, no! I see an innumerable company of the heavenly
host, crying, 'Holy, holy, holy, is the Lord God Almighty'. "
If Wordsworth's words are accepted, and I see no reason not
to accept them, the experience is easily understood, and differs from the commonplace only as *imaging* or truly *imagin-
ing* Druids with extraordinary fullness differs from *thinking
of* Druids, which everyone would do at Stonehenge. The
real importance of the passage, to my mind, lies not in itself,
but in its relation to other poetic experiences of Wordsworth's.
It seems not unlikely that much the same sort of thing frequently took place in varying degrees in his mind, but that
because of obscurity in the experience, or because of the poet's
reticence, it was less distinctly recorded. There was that ash
at Cambridge, for instance; seeing the tree called up "tran-
quil visions" either in his mind or before him—that is, outside
himself. The extent to which the images are externalized is
a matter only of their *vividness,* not of their nature. The analogy with what happened on Salisbury Plain is perfect, the

only difference being that Wordsworth has not chosen to describe the "waking dreams" of the nights at Cambridge in detail.

Perhaps something of the same sort happened at Ullswater. Those severer spirits of Nature who even in 1799 Wordsworth said he believed led him out upon the water and frightened him back again and haunted him afterward by day and night—perhaps they were somehow like the "bright appearances" underneath the ash or the ancient Britons on Salisbury Plain. It may be that the uprising shape of Black Crag against the night sky excited the boy's imagination; it surely excited the boy, but I mean that it called before his mind images which he attributed to the external objects of nature, undefined images which he, being a boy and a primitive pagan, confused with and read into the world about him as awe-inspiring spirits. At any rate, I suggest that this is a possible statement of the boy's experience, and even, when one remembers with what distinctness the man Wordsworth perceived images suggested by the scenes before him, a fairly probable statement. For one thing, it accounts for the aftermath: the awakened or excited images, the "grim shapes," which were the "huge and mighty forms" at once like and unlike living men, survived long after the original stimulation, and insistently preoccupied the poet's mind, with the greater power because only half apprehended.

If there be any truth in this surmise, that Wordsworth was prone to respond to external stimuli with the production of unusually intense images and to externalize these images, that he was, in his own words,

> By sensible impressions not enthrall'd
> But quicken'd, rous'd, and made thereby more apt
> To hold communion with the invisible world,

a clue is afforded to the peculiar type of those experiences which furnished the stuff for his most typical poetry and his most typical beliefs. These experiences, though basically of the same kind, assumed several forms. At one extreme the images wholly usurped and blotted out the external world, as in the vision of the Druids' human sacrifice, or as when Wordsworth crossed the Alps, and Imagination—

> the Power so called
> Through sad incompetence of human speech . . .
> Like an unfathered vapour that enwraps,
> At once, some lonely traveller—

and Wordsworth adds that

> in such strength
> Of usurpation, when the light of sense
> Goes out, but with a flash that has revealed
> The invisible world, doth greatness make abode.

Next to this extreme I should put the times when the images did not displace the outside scene but merely competed with it on a par, as when Wordsworth saw ancient Britons striding across the wold. The next gradation would be the partial blending of the images with natural objects, as at Patter-

dale, or as on those frequent mornings in his boyhood when
Wordsworth left home before daybreak and went

> and sate among the woods
> Alone upon some jutting eminence,
> At the first gleam of dawn-light, when the Vales
> Yet slumbering, lay in utter solitude—
> Oft in these moments such a holy calm
> Would overspread my soul, that bodily eyes
> Were utterly forgotten, and what I saw
> Appeared like something in myself, a dream,
> A prospect in the mind.

Of such moments in his boyhood Wordsworth says in a note
to the "Intimations": "I was often unable to think of external
things as having external existence, and I communed with
all that I saw as something, not apart from, but inherent
in, my own immaterial nature. Many times while going to
school have I grasped at a wall or tree to recall myself from
this abyss of idealism to the reality. At that time I was afraid
of such processes. In later periods of life I have deplored,
as we have all reason today, a subjugation of an opposite
character—

"To that dream-like vividness and splendour which invest
objects of sight in childhood, every one, I believe, if he would
look back, could bear testimony."

That last sentence refers to the sort of experience, at the
other extreme from the blotting out of the sensible world,
which most readers no doubt think of as most typically
Wordsworthian—those times when natural objects are height-

ened and glorified, but not otherwise altered, by the perceiv-
ing mind. Wordsworth himself, referring to his dreamlike
seeing of the vale at dawn, goes on to say:

> I still retained
> My first creative sensibility—
> A plastic power
> Abode with me; a forming hand, at times
> Rebellious, acting in a devious mood;
> A local spirit of his own, at war
> With general tendency, but, for the most,
> Subservient strictly to external things
> With which it communed. An auxiliar light
> Came from my mind, which on the setting sun
> Bestowed new splendour; the melodious birds,
> The fluttering breezes, fountains that run on
> Murmuring so sweetly in themselves, obeyed
> A like dominion, and the midnight storm
> Grew darker in the presence of my eye.

Wordsworth himself wavered in his opinion as to the source
of these transformations. His first impulse seems to have
been to attribute much to nature—originally to the Pres-
ences, Visions, Souls, Powers, genii, familiars, that

> did make
> The surface of the universal earth
> With triumph and delight, with hope and fear,
> Work like a sea.

And he says that he "drank the visionary power" while listening to

> The ghostly language of the ancient earth.

And he never forsook the belief that nature was informed
and animated by a spirit which at times spontaneously produced effects analagous to the effects worked by human
imagination. He was always convinced of a parallelism between man's mind and nature.

> A balance, an ennobling interchange
> Of action from without and from within;
> The excellence, pure function, and best power
> Both of the object seen, and eye that sees.

To this theme he dedicated his great work:

> How exquisitely the individual Mind
> (And the progressive powers perhaps no less
> Of the whole species) to the external World
> Is fitted:—and how exquisitely, too—
> Theme this but little heard of among men—
> The external World is fitted to the Mind;
> And the creation (by no lower name
> Can it be called) which they with blended might
> Accomplish:—this is our high argument.

In other words, although he did his best to make his creed
conform to the demands of reason and common sense and
Anglican piety, he would never consent to admit that all his
most profound and intense experiences were baseless fabrics
without foundation in reality. Surely he was right in this
refusal; but I cannot myself agree to his explanation. I should
as lief believe that the material frame of things had many
souls as one, and while certainly I think that Wordsworth's
experiences had their thoroughly real foundations, I suspect

that he mistook the nature and even the locality of those foundations.

When Wordsworth beheld nature enhanced, may not his mind have been going through essentially the same process as when nature caused him to see visions? That is, may it not be that then too the stimuli summoned before his mind images which he promptly externalized—but which, on the occasions of which we are speaking, he did not apprehend as distinct from external things?—which, in other words, he completely fused with the objects which had called them forth?—thus attributing to the objects qualities which properly pertained to the images, vivifying the objects with a kind of semihuman animation, always with a preternatural vividness and power and glory? Wordsworth, as the preceding quotations sufficiently testify, was often half conscious of what he was doing—he knew that an "auxiliar light" came from his mind; but he could never bring himself wholly to relinquish a belief in some sort of spiritual presence in nature, to admit that what he so delighted to find there was altogether exported and transveyed from himself, for the reason, I take it, that to have admitted this would for him have been to impugn the worth of the experiences themselves. He had found first deities and later God in nature, and to have confessed that he found divinity there because he had put it there himself would have been to question the existence of the divine.

As to why some images should have been wholly fused

with their external stimuli, others partially, and some not at all, I should say there is a double answer. First, a dim and vague image can be more readily fused than a distinct and detailed one, and second, the closer the resemblance of image to external object the more easily they combine. The Druids were seen with remarkable clarity and minuteness, and had no likeness to any objects actually present on Salisbury Plain. The other extreme cannot well be illustrated because the process of blending loses the image in the object—but we shall make an effort as best we can to detect a few of these images in Wordsworth's report of his experiences. No one, I may say, is likely to succeed in this detection whose mind is not in some degree similar to Wordsworth's in its way of working—whose mind, that is, does not quickly respond by the production of images.

What pictures are evoked by the following lines?

> Earth has not anything to show more fair:
> Dull would he be of soul who could pass by
> A sight so touching in its majesty:
> This City now doth, like a garment, wear
> The beauty of the morning; silent, bare,
> Ships, towers, domes, theatres, and temples lie
> Open unto the fields, and to the sky;
> All bright and glittering in the smokeless air.
> Never did sun more beautifully steep
> In his first splendour, valley, rock, or hill;
> Ne'er saw I, never felt, a calm so deep!
> The river glideth at his own sweet will:
> Dear God! the very houses seem asleep;
> And all that mighty heart is lying still!

A picture of many buildings, of course, and a river with ships upon it, all in bright sunlight. Is that all? I can speak only for myself, and say that I see the City also as a majestic figure, a woman's figure, clothed in a shining garment of beauty and light, half reclining beside slowly flowing water, with the Sun pouring down his flood of light upon her. And when I read the lines,

> It is a beauteous evening, calm and free,
> The holy time is quiet as a Nun
> Breathless with adoration; the broad sun
> Is sinking down in its tranquillity;
> The gentleness of heaven broods o'er the Sea:
> Listen! the mighty Being is awake,
> And doth with his eternal motion make
> A sound like thunder—everlastingly,

I see, besides the scene itself and the figure of the nun kneeling in worship, other shapes, more dim and vast, one a shape of quiet and gentle tenderness, outspread, brooding over the face of the waters, the other, the mighty Being, old Ocean himself.

Hidden behind both sonnets, implicit in them, and giving them a major portion of their force, I find forms such as Blake might have drawn; whether anyone else finds them there I cannot say. Yet surely in some minds such lines as these always awaken responses

> Which through the deep and labyrinthine soul,
> Like echoes through long caverns, wind and roll.

The "Ode on the Intimations of Immortality" abounds in lines which have this magical power:

> The Moon doth with delight
> Look round her when the heavens are bare—
> The cataracts blow their trumpets from the steep—
> The Winds come to me from the fields of sleep,—

which certainly, in spite of Hales and Dowden, is not equivalent to "The winds come to me from over the yet reposeful slumbering countryside," but is better illustrated by being set beside these lines of an American writer, based upon Indian myth:

> Winds are the most ancient of Beings,
> Soft winds are the Ancients of All!
> Wherefore breathing
> Is the first of the motions of life,
> Breath-bodies are the first of living things!

Yet to say that Wordsworth's line means "The breath of life comes to me from the realm of dream and vision," or that it evokes mysterious Blake-like figures, would be as partial as to say that it conveys a picture of fields in the country early on a windy morning: it fuses all these, and more, in the words

> The Winds come to me from the fields of sleep.

In the Ode, as we all know, Wordsworth tells how in his childhood every natural object appeared to him transfigured by a celestial light, a visionary gleam, a dreamlike glory and freshness, and how this supernal radiance has disappeared;

by way of explanation, he suggests that the splendor has its source in the child's shadowy recollections of that imperial palace whence he came, and that these memories die out in later life—and he also says that they

> Are yet the fountain-light of all our day,
> Are yet a master-light of all our seeing.

If I were to make a literal transcription of Wordsworth's view, I should say that as a child he had a remarkable ability to respond to natural objects by the production of inner images, that by forthwith blending these images with nature he imparted a transcendent magical aspect, and that as he grew older he gradually lost the capacity for such responses. I question Wordsworth's argument for preëxistence, and also his belief that everyone has such capacities as his and that these die out in middle age. The points in the ode which seem to me most worth pursuing in exploring poetic experience are that the images are innate, that the evocation of them produces a kind of ecstasy, and that they are fraught with meaning and constitute the "master-light of all our seeing," so that to be in touch with them is to read "the eternal deep,"

> Haunted forever by the eternal mind.

A curious parallel with Wordsworth's Ode and a no less curious divergence from it may be found in an essay of Charles Lamb's, "Witches and Other Night Fears." Lamb tells how the nights of his childhood were made miserable by a picture which he often saw in the daytime, a picture of the Witch of Endor raising up Samuel. But, he says, to the picture he owed not the "midnight terrors" themselves, but only "the shape and manner of their visitations": "Had I never met with the picture, the fears would have come self-pictured in some shape or other." And he adds:

> Gorgons, and Hydras, and Chimaeras—dire stories of Celaeno and the Harpies—may reproduce themselves in the brain of superstition—but they were there before. They are transcripts, types—*the archetypes are in us, and eternal.*—These terrors—date beyond body—or, without the body, they would have been the same.
>
> That the kind of fear here treated of is purely spiritual—that it is strong in proportion as it is objectless upon earth—that it predominates in the period of sinless infancy—are difficulties, the solution of which might afford some probable insight into our ante-mundane condition, and a peep at least into the shadow land of preëxistence.

Lamb's are shapes of terror only, and Wordsworth's more often of delight than terror—Lamb's are entirely self-generated, "objectless upon earth," whereas Wordsworth's are called forth by external objects and almost though not quite always read into the world outside. But the writers agree in referring these phenomena to childhood, and to a basis that is innate. Wordsworth relates them to "the eternal deep," "the eternal mind"; Lamb, in the most interesting sentence of the essay, states: "The archetypes are in us, and eternal."

That man is in touch with two worlds and that in their disparity lies his affliction is no novel idea, nor that in harmonizing or uniting the two he finds his joy and consummation; neither has it escaped remark that from the achievement of this union poetry derives much of its power. To be sure, theorists according to their private bias tend to lay greater stress on one world or the other: Max Eastman in *The Enjoyment of Poetry* makes the peculiarity of the poetic attitude consist in aliveness to the outside world; Prescott, in *The Poetic Mind,* in inner experience, in the gift of phantasy. Prescott, however, comes as close as anyone to equal recognition of both claims:

Indeed except in purely subjective illusion, which would not give rise to poetry of value, there must be a reaction of the visionary mind upon nature, and a fusion of external and internal elements. ... Either element taken alone is impotent; nature, until subjected to the mind, is but an "inanimate, cold world"; the mind, without its start and base in nature, will produce only empty and disordered dreams. ... In poetic vision, the sight of a present object, or a sound, or a smell, perhaps a most ordinary one, will start the associations, forming the nucleus, and becoming phantasmo-genetic. But the external experience may be much more than a starting-point; it may be the larger element, while the subjective modification is relatively slight. And so there may be all degrees in the combination of the two factors, from a very slight making over of the external reality to a complete one, amounting to a new subjective creation.

Prescott, in analyzing the "reaction of the visionary mind upon nature," gives a perfect account of the Wordsworthian process; whether, however, he is justified in attributing the same process, as he seems to do, to all poets is questionable. Surely we had better assume that there may be many ways of fusing the two elements, of amalgamating the outer and the inner worlds. When Plato found himself face to face with a matter of which he knew too little to speak in literal terms, he resorted to metaphor and myth; and I am following Plato's example in referring to an outer and an inner world. Undeniably the phrase is a figure of speech; but perhaps it is a figure of speech which metaphorically expresses a truth. The "external world" is of course the physical or material world perceived by means of organs of sense. Of it we may know little, but our acquaintance with it is the closest intimacy and most thorough understanding compared with our black ignorance of the other, the "inner world."

For the moment, the "inner world" may be taken as the world of images. To few people is it utterly unknown; most men can at least call to mind memory images of some sort or other, and many can reform them into new combinations, or, on the basis of what they have sensibly perceived, can make shift at need to image for themselves a unicorn or a centaur, Pegasus, or Bottom wearing the ass's head. And the majority make nightly incursions into the image realm in the form of dreams. Even the daydream or reverie is common to the degree that its existence can scarcely be denied—yet its nature and quality and above all its range may be misapprehended. Possibly to most men "daydream" signifies a series of hazy, evanescent, and unrelated pictures which float before the mind and which usually have to do with pleasant memories or pleasant anticipations or impossible wishes. But a reverie may be much more: it may be as clear and full-bodied as the intensest dream, in it one may touch and I daresay smell and taste, as well as see, may hear sounds and carry on conversations with persons—in short, it is possible through reverie, as through dream, to enter a world of images as complete and apparently as autonomous and independent as the material universe. To anyone who should feel uneasy at this possibility or inclined to call such waking dreamers madmen, it should be said that the two worlds are mistaken only by the insane, and that while the records of these experiences, these explorations into the realm of image, are indisputable, two points must be kept in mind: as some are born blind and deaf and thus unfitted to investigate the external world, so some seem to lack the capacity to observe the imaginary world; and again, whereas of late men have pursued intelligent inquiries into the physical universe, such inquiries into the other universe have seldom as yet been undertaken at all. For the most part we are dependent upon the accounts of dreams and upon reports of such observers as Bunyan and Blake—of men to whom visions came spontaneously. Such visionaries have been prone to take their *visitations* as private *revelations* savoring of the supernatural or miraculous, and men in general have been too quick to dismiss them as idle aberrations. Both these attitudes I think mistaken.

It is easy and natural for some men to turn at will from the outside world and to enter into the world of phantasy, nor is there anything necessarily abnormal in the moments when that world obtrudes itself upon one's attention. In other

words, the inner world, like the outer, is continuous and real;
the inner flux, like the outer, goes on whether one heeds it
or not; and as in dream, reverie, and phantasy one forgets
the external and yet it persists, so in most waking moments
one ceases to attend to the image realm and yet it also persists,
merely waiting to be attended to, and sometimes forcing
itself upon one's notice. Moreover, immaterial and incorporeal
as images may be, they are real—they indubitably are often
present to the mind—just as dreams are real since indubitably
people have them. Phantasy and vision are neither morbid
nor miraculous; nor need they be unprofitable. If they often
are so, likewise many men's observations of the material
world are of very little profit: it depends upon the observer.
If we assent to Max Eastman's dictum that "the essence of
the poetic temper" is "a wish to experience life and the
world," we ought not, like him, too hastily assume that the
experience of one world is more genuine or important or valuable than of the other. As things and events range from the
most trivial to the most momentous, so there are classes and
degrees of images which need to be discriminated. Three
sorts, with infinite gradations between them, are common
enough in dreams: those which are accurately reproduced
from waking experience, those which are familiar enough in
most respects but strangely altered or transfigured, and those
which we are able to derive from no external source and
which carry with them an effect of something preternatural—
of eerie mystery, of joy or beauty, of sublimity, terror, or awe.

To these Shelley refers as
> those subtle or fair spirits,
> Whose homes are the dim caves of human thought,

and also as

> Shapes that haunt thought's wildernesses

and when he says that

> Shapeless sights come wandering by,
> The ghastly people of the realm of dream.

To these Lamb refers, and unless I am altogether mistaken, Wordsworth too, as inborn, and as especially familiar in child-hood. Of these Lamb says that "they are transcripts, types— the archetypes are in us, and eternal"—or, in Wordsworth's words,

> Characters of the great Apocalypse,
> The types and symbols of eternity.

If Lamb's statement were accepted as literal truth, pos-sibly it might prove a clue which would lead to interesting speculations; it might even prove helpful toward under-standing certain kinds of poetic experience—and one of the best tests for such an idea is to try to put it to use. One con-clusion to which the conjecture would guide us is that two sources should be postulated for the images which constitute the image world. One of these is of course the objects of the material world: upon them many images are obviously based, directly or indirectly. But Lamb suggests that there may be another source or basis in what he calls archetypes, and I pro-

pose to assume that some classes of images partake of the
archetypal character. These are the more remote from the
physical world, from the commonplace of everyday life; their
derivation from external experience is extremely difficult if
not impossible to trace; they impress us with their unfamili-
arity, their strangeness. Indeed the peculiar mark of the
archetypal image is that it is preternatural, supernal; whether
beautiful, weird, dreadful, or sublime, it has magical quality,
enchantment—what is called *mana*. The best word, after all,
is *preternatural*. Such images are often if not always more
or less *mythic* in kind, and serve as one link, if links are
needed, between poetry and myth, and make possible the
interpretation of the one by the other. They are often surrounded by an aura of strong emotion, even of ecstasy, often
symbolic, charged with implicit meaning.

The archetypes themselves should be thought of as inborn
patterns or engrams imprinted in the very ground of the
mind—perhaps, for all I know, as precipitates or deposits of
racial experience, so that to be in touch with them is

> to read the eternal deep,
> Haunted forever by the eternal mind.

That—because of their immemorial associations—may be
why they are accompanied by feelings so powerful, and why
they are so full of significance as to constitute

> ... the fountain-light of all our day,
> ... a master-light of all our seeing.

Whether or not they can ever be apprehended in their purity
I dare not hazard a guess, though it looks as if they had been
seen with only the slightest tincture derived from physical
reality by Blake and Shelley and by others gifted with a mind

> that broods
> Over the dark abyss, intent to hear
> Its voices issuing forth to silent light
> In one continuous stream.

I incline however to suspect that, like the shades whom
Odysseus met in the underworld, they must drink material blood before they can speak—that Shelley was right in
exclaiming

> If the abysm
> Could vomit forth its secrets! But a voice
> Is wanting, the deep truth is imageless—

in brief, that what I have called an archetypal image is never
the archetype itself, but at best a fusion in varying propor-
tions of the archetype with an image derived from the outside
world.

The distinctive mark of poetic experience is the uniting
of the external and the archetypal, and there are as many
varieties of poetic experiences as there are ways of effecting
this combination. In trying to describe the mode most characteristic of Wordsworth, in which the initial component is
a material object or scene into which the poet reads the archetypal images excited by what he perceives, I have not meant
to imply that all Wordsworth's poetic experiences followed

this form—and still less that those of other poets follow it.
For one thing, it is often impossible to tell from a poem itself
what innumerable experiences of all sorts have gone to its
making; autobiographical poems like *The Prelude* are rare,
and poems the inception of which is recounted in letters,
diaries, memoirs, and the like are few. Yet the only feasible procedure seems to be to take what evidence we have,
and from it to make guesses at what we do not know. Fortunately, Wordsworth is not the only poet for whom we can
reconstruct with some assurance the basic experiences which
underlie his poetry; and to turn to these other writers is to
find at once that not all poets follow Wordsworth's pattern.

On the afternoon of October 25, 1819, Shelley was walking in a wood that skirts the Arno near Florence. A strong
wind was blowing from the west, scattering the brilliant
leaves of autumn. Soft and mild as it was, it disturbed and
exhilarated him. The thin clouds streaming across the sky
foretold a storm, and at sunset it broke—a tempest of hail
and rain, with tremendous thunder and lightning. But before Shelley was driven away he had conceived a poem and
had written most of it. In the poem one would expect to find
some description of the scene which prompted it—and so, in
a sense, one does, in scattered phrases here and there: the
dead leaves fly past, yellow, and black, and pale, and hectic
red, and the winged seeds whirl about; the blue sky is half
covered with blown loose clouds; the storm approaches,

about to burst in black rain and fire and hail; and the forest and all resound with the tumult of mighty harmonies. Yet from the poem few will get a real picture of the scene, and for a good reason. For the wind is Autumn's life breath; the leaves are ghosts fleeing in pestilence-stricken multitudes from an enchanter; the clouds are angels of rain and lightning; a fierce maenad appears, her bright hair uplifted from her head and streaming through the firmament; a sea-blue deity lies sleeping under the bay of Baiae beside a pumice isle, and in his dreams he sees old palaces and towers

> Quivering within the wave's intenser day,
> All overgrown with azure moss and flowers.

The waves of the Atlantic are cleft into chasms; beneath them on the ocean floor the sea-blooms and the oozy woods *hear* the wind's *voice, tremble,* and *despoil themselves* of their sapless foliage. Image within image, like wheel within wheel: and all mythic and magical, primeval, preternatural— archetypal. No wonder most would think that the afternoon beside the Arno is not described at all, the airy moths and hummingbirds of Shelley's mind flit so thickly about the perception which has attracted them. Shelley's head was always a hive humming with bees of fancy, and such a scene as the evening near Florence was a waxen frame of comb no sooner placed in the hive than the bees clustered upon it and filled it with their honey.

Shelley perceives the objects about him, the external scene;

these perceptions elicit the archetypal images and are speedily blended with and incorporated in the images, and assimilated to them—leaves and clouds turn into ghosts and angels
and maenads with floating hair,—the result being, not as
with Wordsworth a cloud with attributes of a maenad, but
rather a maenad with attributes of cloud. These images, furthermore, are Shelley's, are in a sense parts of himself; he
inclined to identify them with himself: no sooner has he felt
and heard the wind and seen things blown along by it than
he imagines a wild spirit which *is* the wind, akin to some
wild force in himself that often drives in tumult before it
throngs of thoughts and visions and dreams: if he were a
dead leaf—a swift cloud—a wave—he could share the impulse
of this strength—at times he has shared it, has been "tame-
less, and swift, and proud"—in a way, he *is* a spirit like the
wind—why cannot they be one?

> Be thou, Spirit fierce,
> My spirit! Be thou me, impetuous one!

So, by first identifying the image with himself, Shelley tends
to identify with himself the object which called forth the
image and was fused into it; tends not to go forth and lose
himself in the external scene, but to draw it into himself:
"Be thou me!" I do not say that such is Shelley's habitual
or commonest process; merely that he follows it not only in
the "Ode to the West Wind," but also in "To a Skylark" and
possibly in the "Lines Written among the Euganean Hills"
and "The Cloud," and perhaps in others.

The crucial point of the process is the moment when sense-perceptions and images are fused, for one or the other must conquer. Which is to be victorious seems to depend on whether the poet's bent is stronger to externalize or to internalize. Wordsworth, in what are generally thought his most characteristic moments, gives the prize to the material world—Shelley, at least at times, to the image. Shelley's images are invigorated by drinking the blood of material objects; Wordsworth's objects are glorified and transfigured by imbibing the ichor of the archetypes. Wordsworth says once:

> —and lo! as I looked up,
> The Moon hung naked in a firmament
> Of azure without cloud, and at my feet
> Rested a silent sea of hoary mist;

and Shelley,

> That orbed maiden with white fire laden
> Whom mortals call the moon,
> Glides glimmering o'er my fleece-like floor
> By the midnight breezes strewn.

Wordsworth's propensity is to externalize images, Shelley's to internalize objects.

These, then, are two modes of amalgamating inner and outer, two varieties of poetic experience—for I do not question Prescott's conclusion that the secret of poetic experience is "a fusion of external and internal elements," though I prefer to say of physical world and archetypal image. No doubt there are many ways of achieving this fusion; for example, many poetic experiences begin with the apprehending not of external things but of archetypal images. Sometimes, when the image presents itself to the mind, it is read into or incorporated in external reality, sometimes external reality is read into it—perhaps Coleridge and Keats respectively might afford examples of these processes. However that may be, it is enough at present to remark the need of both elements. Mere observation of the outer world tends to be matter-of-fact and photographic, and while no doubt it may occasion strong feeling and strenuous thought, and while poetry based upon it may have many values, probably nothing in the initial experience itself would be called poetic. On the other hand, mere phantasy, mere reception of images apparently unrelated to the material universe, though this experience would more commonly be thought poetic, and though it too might awaken thought and feeling, is likely to result in poetry that is filmy, flimsy, lacking in substance and moment. When both the vital components are present, the experience evinces extraordinary power and value. From its physical constituent it derives body, stuff, robust vigor, the pungency and sting of actuality; from the archetypal images, its magical potency, its symbolic and mythic quality, its inexhaustible significance, and its grip upon the roots of our being. Nor is this all. A Frenchman once said: "Do you know what it is that makes man the most suffering of all creatures? It is . . . that he is torn asunder, not by four horses as in the horrible old times, but between two worlds." His body can find no satisfaction in the incorporeal realm of image, and in the heedless realm of matter he has come to feel "like a motherless child a long way from home." In either order of reality man's plight is bitter. Only when the two orders are fused in poetic experience does man find himself at home in a world fit for human habitation. Nor need one jump at the inference that in the fusion there is anything illusory, for it may be that in their poetic moments men remarry what they should never have put asunder, that the two orders are not so disparate as they look. At any rate, to live in the two worlds as one is to free oneself from the inadequacies of both, is to find a full and complete experience. And when, furthermore, as in the great poems, this experience is wrought and molded to those forms of perfection which man can contemplate but never realize in his own life, he comes closest to escape from his tragic predicament and to fulfillment of the destiny which he wishes were his.

[1930]

Literature as Action

P ERHAPS we are most accustomed nowadays to considering a book in terms of its author: we ask how it expresses
his personality, or how it illustrates the age to which he
belonged. But I suggest that the primary question should be,
"What is its relation to us, to its living readers?" There is
nothing novel in this question: "What does literature do to
and for its readers?" is the stock question of all classical criticism. But I wish to go a little further, beyond the effect on
the isolated individual reader, and to inquire whether the
most important thing about a book is, not its relation to some
past age in which it was produced, but rather its relation to
this present age in which it is read. I ask you for a while
to think of literature as a living force acting on the present
world—that is, as a form of social action.

We should expect, should we not, to care most for those
books which best meet our most vital needs—that is, the most
vital needs of the present world? But what are they? You can
hardly get two people to agree. One of the commonest answers might be, "Need of values"—that is, of something to
care about and to live for. And there is much in this answer,
but I think we shall arrive at a better solution if, instead of
seeking it in the individual's mind, we look outside, at society, where we find the individual's difficulties written large

in social conflicts. My own explanation would be that the
present is a time of unusual and profound social disharmony,
which I should explain thus.

In most respects society has become collective, tightly knit
together, every member closely interdependent on every
other, most of our undertakings and activities involving vast
coöperation. But in certain respects it has remained individualistic, notably in control or power, in certain aspects of our
property system, and above all in the distribution of profits.
The crux of the situation, then, as I see it, is the struggle between two societies, the old individualistic one which is dying, and the new rising collective one which is growing
stronger and stronger. But because of inertia or cultural lag
our minds belong largely to the past; mentally we are incor-
rigible individualists. Many of us can no longer accept the
old values; but neither have we accepted the new. Here, I
admit, is a guess in the dark—but if we looked for our satisfaction in successful social functioning, might we not feel the
lack of values less acutely? Only—how is one to attain successful social functioning in the existing state of affairs?

You may wonder what these questions have to do with
literature. For is not literature a fine art, and does it not therefore lift us out of the turmoil into a serener air? Is it not a
form of contemplation, disinterested and detached? In a way,
I think it is, sometimes, a kind of disinterested contemplation,
though I doubt whether it is detached. And is not the fruit
of contemplation sooner or later to issue in action? A detached

contemplation of human struggle, wrong, and suffering, with a secret smile of aesthetic pleasure at the spectacle, may befit the gods, but surely it is too godlike an attitude to befit mere human beings.

Literature does act upon us, in a thousand ways. Among other things, it affirms values; writers make us care about things, feel about them, as they do. And usually they are quite explicit about it; they tell us outright what they like or dislike. The great exception may seem to be Shakespeare, and I confess that this quality in him—this ability to give both sides, to give the devil his due—is one of the chief marks of his greatness, his superiority to other writers. Yet I do not believe in Shakespeare's detachment; of course I shall not try to state his view of life, but I think one is discernible in his plays, and I should say that almost always the feelings of the reader are quite clearly directed for or against certain traits and actions of his characters. While I admit that I can get examples more easily from other writers, I do not think Shakespeare can be set up as exception to what I have to say.

One of the functions of literature as of all the arts is too often overlooked: the communication of power, the enhancement of energy. It leaves us more alive, stronger; we feel that virtue has come into us. This heightening of vitality or increase of life accounts in large measure for the joy and delight that art gives us. But the point I wish to stress is that literature not only gives us this augmented power, but, by the values it asserts, directs it. All good writers do this, but most of them act only on part, often a small part, of one; the best or greatest, however, act so upon all of one, on the whole man. They heighten and harmonize and direct our power to think, to feel, to imagine—and to will and to act. They intensify and enlarge our consciousness and awareness. And they do all this to us not as isolated individuals only, but as social beings, for by their own awareness of personal and social relations they enhance ours.

I grant that most literature does much less. In fact, I should say that hardly since Milton wrote *Samson Agonistes* has a whole man appeared in literature, either as character or as author. One after another, important elements have been dropped out: the will expressing itself, first in social action, then in any kind of action; the sense of human relationships; the intellect expressing itself in coherent thought; until even thinking and consciousness themselves have been attacked. More and more we have suffered from a race of solitary, will-less, do-nothing, unthinking heroes and writers. The process has reached its extremity in certain poets and characters who pose as lonely souls against the stars and suffer helplessly in a welter of emotion and imagination.

But this extreme is rare; most literature does affirm some positive values. And this brings me back to literature in relation to the present world, as a form of social action in the existing social situation. When we look at literature from this point of view, we observe, first of all, that, though the values which literature asserts are many and varied, though it turns

the energies it arouses in many different directions, it almost
never turns them toward the values upon which our society
was founded: acquisition, and the struggle of individuals for
profits. If it were taken at all seriously, practically all literature would be to some extent subversive. Furthermore, we
must recognize that many of these values are inappropriate
to our situation; for us they are not values. The cults of hedonism, of escape, of isolated individualism, or of no values, of
futility, despair, are all denials of the whole man; even the
best of them, the cult of detached and disinterested contemplation, is so, if we believe that the man who does not act
is incomplete. If there is anything in my guess that our most
vital need is to adapt ourselves to the new rising collective
side of society and to find our satisfaction in successful social
functioning, it would seem to follow that the best literature
for us is that which not only most heightens our energy, but
which also brings the whole man into play, into action, as a
social being. For the following reasons.

The major conflict of our time, I said, is between two
groups of forces. The first, which is still in control and rules
our world, derives from the economic individualism of the
past; it is based upon the principle of the survival of the fittest
in the struggle for profits. Because they belong to the past,
these forces resist change; they are forces of reaction and re-
pression. In literature, any of the many cults of inaction plays
into their hands. But, above all, these forces are allied with
the literary cult of violence, force, cruelty, and death, the cult

of instinctive action, of unconsciousness, which opposes rational thinking and humane feelings and positive social functioning; the cult of incompleteness and self-mutilation.

The other group of forces, which derives from the collective side of our society, the rising, growing, but not yet dominant side, is directed rather toward the future and toward progressive social coöperative activity. It stresses, not the fight of individuals for profits, but rather the importance of social function with suitable reward. Because it is constructive and not repressive, this side needs all the knowledge and thought and awareness it can get, and, because it is not in control, all the disciplined will leading to vigorous social action. It can use and must get the whole man, at his best.

In this great conflict impartiality is impossible and undesirable. Any man who denies the acquisitive values—and who was ever so blind as to go into literature as teacher, critic, or poet with the hope of piling up profits?—anyone who aims at wholeness, or who would like to play a positive role and function in society to the best of his ability, must choose the second side. Therefore the best literature for us is the sort that best conditions us to do so—which means, since the second side has as yet received no adequate literary expression in our time and tongue, the classics, those books which have generally been recognized as the best and greatest. They will help us to do what we can toward the creation of the new society, a society that will not deny so many human values and maintain such inhuman ones; that will help us, not by specific propaganda, but by activating the whole man and turning him toward that completer and more fully satisfactory life which can be obtained for himself and others only through fundamental social change. If you call that propaganda, all right: do we not believe in propaganda for knowledge, intelligence, consciousness, understanding, for disciplined will and imagination and feeling, and for action carrying these out in valuable social functioning, with faith in the outcome?

Literature as action, then, as I see it, is a conditioning to play as valuable a part as possible in existing society, always looking forward toward the creation of the new society—not propaganda for a particular program, but a conditioning of the whole man. Even though we do not claim that we know all the answers, we can look at literature and interpret and criticize it—and perhaps produce it—in the spirit of Blake's lines—

> I will not cease from mental fight,
> Nor shall my sword sleep in my hand,
> Till we have built Jerusalem
> In England's green and pleasant land.

[1937]